Daily Happy Living

How to Use the Joycentrix System to
Enable Us to Be Happy Each Day despite
the Challenges We Face Daily

Gopi Menon

PARTRIDGE
A Penguin Random House Company

Library of Congress Control Number:		2014937432
ISBN:	Hardcover	978-1-4828-9625-1
	Softcover	978-1-4828-9624-4
	Ebook	978-1-4828-9253-6

To order additional copies of this book, contact
Toll Free 800 101 2657 (Singapore)
Toll Free 1 800 81 7340 (Malaysia)
orders.singapore@partridgepublishing.com
www.partridgepublishing.com/singapore

CONTENTS

DEDICATION

This book is dedicated to the memory of my mother. My mother was a traditional homemaker but untraditional in her thinking, perhaps because she was good at languages and was an avid reader. Having been educated in Kerala, India, she could read and write Sanskrit, Malayalam, and English.

When she came over to Malaysia to start a new life after she married my father, who worked as a manager in a rubber estate, she studied Tamil too. Because of her background in Sanskrit and Malayalam, she was able to master Tamil well enough within four months to start teaching at the Tamil school in the estate.

Her favorite hobby was reading. She loved to read religious and philosophical books that she hoped would explain the meaning of life. I loved to hear her read these stories out loud to me (including the Indian epics *Ramayana* and *Mahabharata*), even though I kept interrupting her with questions at every turn.

She was the one with whom I had my most early discussions about life, living, God, heaven, hell, and so on. One good trait my mother had was that she always encouraged my questions no matter how perplexing they were.

Even if she found my questions unanswerable, she never told me, "Stop asking such questions," as many mothers would have done in exasperation. Instead she would just say, "Son, I don't know the answer to that, but I believe that one day you may come up with the answer yourself!"

Decades later I seem to have come up with some answers to my early questions about life, living, happiness, God, religion, and so on. Thus, this book is dedicated with love, gratitude, and respect to my mother, without whom this book would never have been written.

PREFACE

Throughout my childhood, my teenage years, and my adulthood, I have been absolutely confused and disappointed with the traditional methods for achieving happiness taught to us by our well-meaning but ill-informed parents, ancient religious teachers, as well as many impractical philosophers!

My problem as a child was that I was too trusting and really believed what these people told me about life, reality, this world, and the hereafter. So I tried to follow the advice given by them faithfully, and yet I found myself unable to achieve many things that I wanted to. I was unhappy! When I questioned them about this, the replies given were quite unhelpful. These included the following:

- *Just accept your problems because it is only God testing you!* (I used to wonder, *When will the testing ever end?*)

- *It is just fate or bad karma from your past lifetime. You have to just accept it!* Then I would ask "If I can't do anything to change my so-called karma, then why do you ask me to pray? Why do you ask me to be good, honest, unselfish, and so on if I am still destined to suffer?" It did not make any sense to me.

- *You are just a pawn in a game played by the gods! You are merely an actor on the stage of life, and you have no choice but to do what the director tells you.* Then I would query, "If I am just a pawn or an actor, then why do you say that I have been given free will and *choice* in my actions? If I am free, then I cannot be a pawn being manipulated by others!"

I am sure that you too have come across such statements and found them incredibly confusing and illogical. Some people tell you to turn to religion for answers. But the repeated refrains you hear from all religions is this:

> The world is an unhappy place to be in. There is a better place for you in your afterlife—but only if you live with guilt (you being a sinner) and suffer enough in this life. Also you must follow our prescriptions faithfully. If you do not, you will end up in a place worse than this world!

The sad thing is that when we are 'brainwashed' from a very young age with such ideas, we grow up accepting them and believing them—even if these ideas are totally irrational and aren't validated with a shred of proof! We unquestioningly accept and believe what our parents say because we love and respect them so much. Furthermore, when these ideas are repeated day in and day out, we tend to internalize these ideas and make them a habit. Thus, the child may grow up to be well educated and even get a doctorate, but he or she is still unable to think independently when it comes to these old ideas!

This was the problem I too faced as a child. The only difference was that from an early age I loved to question my parents and my teachers about everything. I must have made their lives miserable with my incessant and often unanswerable questions.

When I was just seven years old, I remember my mother telling me why we must learn to control our desires. She said that according to Hindu philosophy, "Desire is the starting point of all sorrow! If you had no desires, then you would not have to undergo any suffering."

This seemed illogical to me. *If we did not have any desire, then we would not be motivated to do anything, and we would never achieve anything.*

So I remember asking, "Mother, do you want to attain 'moksha'—i.e. go to heaven?"

She replied, "Of course!"

Then I asked her, "Isn't that a desire—this wanting to go to heaven? So how can you say that having a desire is bad?"

To which my mother (instead of telling me to stop asking such questions, as most mothers would have done) said, "Maybe you will find out the truth someday." And I think I have, after more than five decades—a truth that I hope to reveal in this book.

While I was in my teens, I was encouraged to continue my questioning from the most unlikely of sources—a Tamil movie! I say unlikely because normally a Tamil movie is often pure escapism, consisting of a three-hour-long hotchpotch of drama, love, action, tragedy, comedy, and several songs. Thus, it is very rare to find inspiration from one such movie.

However, in this particular movie there was a sketch about Socrates performed by the legendary Tamil actor, Sivaji Ganesan, in his own inimitable way! Sivaji Ganesan was the doyen of Tamil cinema who was exceptional at speaking the language. The words just rolled off his tongue so poetically and with so much power that I remember thinking: "Even though Socrates must have spoken in Greek, I doubt if he could have matched the oratorical skills of this actor, who was speaking in Tamil!"

Anyway, that observation by itself is not all that unusual. Remember that most famous of speeches by Mark Antony in the play Julius Caesar by Shakespeare that begins, "Friends, Romans, countrymen . . .—" That speech is in English and not Roman or Latin as it should have been originally.

Whatever the case, that sketch was a turning point in my life. The sketch was about the last day in the life of Socrates prior to his execution for 'treason' (another word for 'thinking differently from the state'). Just before taking the poison as ordered by the court, Socrates gave the following advice to his young disciples: "Always question everything. Ask: What? Why? Why not? How? What if? before you accept anything as true."

That one sentence is perhaps the motivation that gave me the courage to question age-old beliefs that were considered sacrosanct and beyond question. It started me on the search for answers as to why happiness was so elusive in this world, and that search has culminated in this book, *Daily Happy Living*.

After years of avidly trying to understand happiness and after much introspection and many positive and negative experiences, I seem to have finally stumbled upon the true way to be happy every day of our lives. I personally believe that any philosophy must be of practical use to us in our daily living. Any other type of philosophy is mere dogma and hence worthless.

As such, I am committed to providing the reader with a practical philosophy that sets out the beliefs I espouse at present and the practices I personally use to achieve happy living here and now. I call this philosophy of mine "The Joycentrix System."

The Joycentrix System is a set of beliefs that makes it easier to find happiness in this world. It outlines a simple natural way to make happy living a habit, and it does not consist of spending hours meditating or droning out so-called sacred words or carrying out ritual worship in the hope of receiving happiness.

Best of all, this GOD-given process is quick and easy (but needs focus and commitment on our part) and can be sped up by the technological innovations available at present. The ideas may seem contrarian or controversial to you at first, but if you persevere, you will find the truth embodied in them.

So if you are not afraid to think independently for yourself (instead of just accepting all the old teachings as absolute truth), then you will find this book useful. If you are looking for simple, practical tips that you can use today to make happy living a habit, then you are holding the correct tool in your hand right now.

My primary purpose with this book is to get people to start thinking independently and not depend entirely on other peoples' interpretations—not mine and not even the Buddha's! That is what Buddha himself would have wished too as he has said clearly in the quote below:

> "Believe nothing, no matter where you read it, or who said it (even if I have said it) unless it agrees with your own reason and your own common sense."—Buddha

I have no wish to convert anyone to my point of view, except to state my own views in clear, somewhat forthright terms. Whether the readers wish to adopt these ideas or not is entirely their own GOD-given choice! My present belief is this:

> *"I now accept that everyone is perfect at his or her own level of evolution; hence it makes no sense for me to try to convert anyone to my point of view. Let each one work out his/her own evolutionary path."*

What I believe and want to encourage in each and every one is critical independent thinking, not blind acceptance. This is what GOD has gifted us with—free will and choice to think independently.

I want you, the reader, to be skeptical, to question everything I say and only accept anything if it agrees with your own reason! If my words make sense, then use them with your own particular slant to make sense of the universe!

Here's to free will, independent thinking, and harmonious action!

Gopi Menon
August, 2013

INTRODUCTION

As stated earlier, this book is the culmination of decades of questioning, searching, personal experiences, and deep introspection about happiness. About four years ago I began to share the end result of my lifelong quest (my personal philosophy on how to attain happiness here and now) via my blog, Daily Happy Living. I am gratified and humbled by the good reviews and comments I have received for many of my postings on the blog.

When people wrote to me to say that they had been inspired by some of my posts, I was extremely grateful because I had not really expected such a good response, especially because of the somewhat contrarian ideas I espoused. It is due to the encouragement of such readers that I embarked on writing a book entitled *Daily Happy Living*.

I realize that the ideas in this book about ways to achieve happiness in this life (and perhaps in the afterlife) may seem controversial to most people in the same way that the idea of a round earth would be controversial to those who believed in the flat-earth theory!

However, controversy is often the harbinger of truth! Any new idea is always first considered to be controversial and subject to deep distrust. Then it gradually gains some acceptability. Finally after much debate and evaluation it is then considered to be the truth.

And it is right that this should be so. We should not just accept anything blindly. A little skepticism is good to begin with. But being skeptical does not mean that we should totally avoid considering the new idea or be passionately resistant to it because it may turn out to be a new truth after all.

A classic example of controversy and deep resistance to new thought is the case of Galileo and the church. When Galileo put forth the heliocentric theory (which said the sun was at the center of the solar system and it was the earth went round the sun, rather than the reverse), the Catholic Church was opposed to it saying it contradicted the bible.

In 1633 Galileo was tried by the Inquisition, found suspect of heresy, forced to recant, and spent the rest of his life under house arrest. His only guilt was that he espoused a truth that is commonplace now.

It took three and a half centuries, but in 1992 the church finally vindicated Galileo, the scientist. As reported in the news, in November 1992, Pope John Paul II stated:

> "Thanks to his intuition as a brilliant physicist and by relying on different arguments, Galileo, who practically invented the experimental method, understood why only the sun could function as the centre of the world, as it was then known, that is to say, as a planetary system. The error of the theologians of the time, when they maintained the centrality of the Earth, was to think that our understanding of the physical world's structure was, in some way, imposed by the literal sense of Sacred Scripture."

Thus, controversy is not unusual when we are searching for truth. As long as we remain sensibly skeptical and yet open to new ideas, we can only profit from the exercise.

Benefits of Reading This Book

By reading and applying the principles presented in this book, the reader can expect the following benefits:

1. Learn the truth about happiness and just what causes misery.
2. Learn to choose happiness on a daily basis despite challenging circumstances.
3. Understand the truth about the world and about living in this world.
4. Get a new insight into GOD as a loving and benevolent entity rather than a vindictive and malevolent being.
5. Know the truth about the powers resident in your mind, which you can use to help create happy circumstances.
6. Get a new insight into creation and co-creation
7. Learn to apply the practical happy living tips to create a happier life for yourself and your family.

How This Book Is Structured

This book is separated into five parts as follows:

Part 1 answers the questions "What is happiness?" as well as "Why do we humans seek happiness?"

> *Chapter 1* is devoted to sifting through the myriad (often contradictory) definitions of happiness. We

then realize that these definitions only focus on one aspect of happiness. Hence I have formulated a more complete definition of happiness, one that covers the three most important aspects of the emotion of happiness, namely the physical (or material), mental (or intellectual), as well the spiritual (or soul) aspects.

Chapter 2 answers the other vital question "Why do we humans seek happiness?" The answer may seem surprising to some, but a little thought will show them why it is quite logical.

Part 2 talks about the power of belief, types of beliefs, and wrong beliefs about happiness.

Chapter 3 is all about the power of belief, which is explained using several stories from the past as well as the present about healings and apparent miracles.

Chapter 4 describes the three major types of beliefs, namely intuitive beliefs, adopted beliefs, and acquired beliefs, and this section explains the positive and negative effects of each type.

Chapter 5 gives several examples of wrong beliefs that cause unhappiness and explains how we can get the right beliefs about happiness.

Chapter 6 debunks a few of the popular myths about how to find happiness and exposes the wrong thinking behind those myths. It also shows how the reader can guard against similar untruths about ways to happiness that could prevent them from the very happiness they seek.

Part 3 introduces the Joycentrix System, which is the foundation of my happy living system. It describes my present beliefs about GOD, the world, evolution, the mind, and happiness itself, which allows me to make daily happy living a way of life.

> *Chapter 7* gives a summary of the Joycentrix System and the five cardinal rules of happy living, while *chapters 8 to 12* describe each of these five rules in detail.

Part 4 deals with the practical application of the Joycentrix principles by using several happy living tips.

> *Chapter 13* gives a list of the various happy living tips for easy reference while *chapters 14 to 18* discuss using these tips for solving some of the challenges we face in daily life as given below.
>
> *Chapter 14* is about how we can attain equanimity and peace of mind.
>
> *Chapter 15* is about having happier relationships.
>
> *Chapter 16* is about learning to be grateful for life.
>
> *Chapter 17* is about how to feel upbeat and energized.
>
> *Chapter 18* is about dealing with people.

Part 5 looks at the Joycentrix System in action. It examines case studies of people actually using the happy living tips and benefiting from them.

> *Chapter 19* is about my own experience with the Joycentrix principles.

Chapter 20 tells the story of how a marriage headed for the rocks was saved.

Chapter 21 describes one example of a happiness enhancer.

Note to the Reader

There are certain things that only we can do for ourselves. Happy living is one of those things we cannot outsource! For example if I want to lose weight, I cannot just employ another person to go the gym and expect results! I have to go to the gym and really work out. Similarly just reading this book alone will not make you happy. You must put the principles into practice.

To assist the reader in putting these principles into practice, I have included inspiring messages and practical assignments at the end of certain chapters. If you truly wish to be happy, please ponder the messages and carry out the practical assignments before you proceed to the next chapter!

PART 1

- ❖ What is happiness?

- ❖ Why do we seek happiness?

CHAPTER 1

What Is Happiness?

What is Happiness? Common sense requires that we answer this question before we go into the details of how to achieve happiness. Unfortunately *happiness* is not easily defined. Everyone seems to have his or her version of happiness.

Here are various definitions of happiness:

1. According to Wikipedia, *happiness* is "a mental or emotional state of well-being characterized by positive or pleasant emotions ranging from contentment to intense joy."

2. Per Merriam-Webster's, *happiness* is "a state of well-being and contentment (joy); pleasurable or satisfying experience."

3. And according to Dictionary.com, happiness is "the quality or state of being happy; good fortune; pleasure; contentment; joy."

The following states of mind can also be termed to give rise to happiness: equanimity, serenity, peace of mind, joy, achievement, enjoyment, respect of others, gratitude, appreciation of music and art, and so on.

In fact, when I google *happiness,* I get so many different definitions and sayings about happiness that they make my head spin. Here are just a few examples from the Google world:

- "Happiness is something that you are and it comes from the way you think" (Wayne Dyer)

- "Happiness is essentially a state of going somewhere, wholeheartedly, one-directionally, without regret or reservation" (William H. Sheldon).

- "Happiness is not a reward—it is a consequence" (Robert Ingersoll).

- "Happiness is different from pleasure. Happiness has something to do with struggling and enduring and accomplishing" (George Sheehan).

- "Happiness is not something you experience, it's something you remember" (Oscar Levant).

- "Happiness is not a station you arrive at, but a manner of traveling" (Margaret Lee Runbeck).

- "Happiness is the spiritual experience of living every minute with love, grace and gratitude" (Denis Waitley).

- "Happiness is the meaning and the purpose of life, the whole aim and end of human existence" (Aristotle).

- "Happiness is a habit" (Abraham Lincoln).

The problem with the above definitions is that each of them focuses only on one aspect of happiness and doesn't explain what happiness really is. So I am coming up with my own definition of happiness, which I hope is more satisfactory and complete:

"Happiness is a state of being where we feel good— whether it is because of sensory pleasures, intellectual pleasures, or spiritual pleasures!"

1. Sensory pleasures are those related to our five senses. Consider these examples:
   a. seeing a beautiful sunset
   b. hearing a melodious song
   c. eating a favorite meal/enjoying a drink
   d. smelling a wonderful perfume
   e. hugging, physical intimacy with a loved one, and so on

2. Intellectual pleasures are those related to our intellect and our mind. Consider the following examples:
   a. reading a good book
   b. remembering something pleasant
   c. planning a dream goal
   d. working toward your dream purpose
   e. writing a book, composing music, or painting
   f. appreciating travel, architecture, and so on
   g. going shopping
   h. buying a new car
   i. winning an honor or award

3. Spiritual pleasures are those related to doing something altruistic or just feeling unconditional love. Consider these examples:

    a.   sharing your particular talent, thereby contributing wisdom, cheer, and inspiration through speaking, writing, music, art, architecture, inventions, and so on

    b.   making monetary contributions and volunteering time and effort to help the needy (orphans, the homeless and the aged, the disabled, and so on)

    c.   those moments of unconditional love (e.g., seeing your infant smile, your puppy frolic, and so on)

In all the examples above, although each one of us acts in ways that may seem so different outwardly, the final motivation to action is always *to feel good* and thus to find happiness!

The above examples apply to the vast majority of people who can be considered normal! To complete the picture, however, we need to list some abnormal and negative aspects of feeling good as shown below.

Unfortunately there do exist certain people whose idea of feeling good is somewhat perverted. These people can include the following:

- sadists who feel good seeing others in pain or suffering

- extremists who believe that by killing others they will get to feel good (find happiness) in the afterlife

- martyrs who believe that by killing themselves they will get to feel good (find happiness) in the afterlife

- dictators who feel good only when everybody else feeds their egos by being servile and never daring to cross them

My point in listing these negative examples is just to show that even in these extreme cases, each person is still taking action to feel good within! On a lesser level the alcoholic, the smoker, and the drug addict are all also taking action (however misguided) to feel good; namely to be happy.

As explained in the next chapter, we are all programmed to do what will make us happy, but our bodies are also built to adapt. When someone first tries to smoke, the body will react instantly to repel the smoke by coughing and choking because it definitely does not feel good. However, if we insist on smoking, gradually the body adapts to the smoke and even learns to like it, and then we become addicted to it. The same is true for alcohol and drugs as well as for all the perversions that people get addicted to.

Okay! That is enough of the negative aspects. Let us get back to question "What does genuine happiness mean to the normal majority?" To the majority of us, happiness is anything that gives us a sense of well-being or contentment. Basically I believe there are three types of happiness:

1. **External happiness:** When the pleasure is caused by use of the five senses (as in seeing beautiful scenery, listening to a haunting melody, eating a favorite food, smelling a fine aroma, making love, and so on). This type of happiness is very temporary. For example, we can have a great lunch and enjoy it tremendously, but a few hours later we become hungry and are ready to eat again.

   External happiness is generally a reaction to an outside stimulus in that it depends on external circumstances. Unfortunately many people think that this type of happiness is the only real happiness.

In fact, most people think that they are unhappy because of the following factors:

- lack of money
- bad relationships
- poor health
- lack of career opportunities
- lack of family support

In other words they think that their unhappiness comes from something external to themselves. However, these are only secondary causes. The main causes have all to do with self and lack of self-awareness!

In other words, unhappiness is mainly caused by our own poor thinking, which gives rise to the following:

- being unaware of our feelings
- being unaware of our thoughts
- wrong beliefs about God, life, and the world
- wrong beliefs about willpower and mind power
- not understanding that our minds are under our own control
- believing that we are at the mercy of fate and circumstance
- reacting rather than responding to the behavior of other people
- superstitions

As you can see from the list above, all of these have to do with our own thinking, and our own actions, which we are in full control of! This we can change if we so wish.

Thus, it is not external circumstances or other people who cause us the most unhappiness, but we ourselves—our wrong way of thinking!

(This may seem unbelievable to many readers, but this book is dedicated to proving that statement to be true.)

2. **Internal happiness:** This occurs when the pleasure is caused by the use of our minds (which include the intellect as well as the emotions), especially fond memories of people, stories, songs, our dreams of achievement, and so on.

    This type of happiness is well within our control. As we focus on happy thoughts, we get happy feelings, and we feel good! The reverse is also true. (Focus on sad thoughts, and you become unhappy.)

    However, internal happiness will always supersede external happiness. For example, if you are really unhappy about something internally, you will not enjoy your favorite food or music or even making love!

    The reverse does not work, but people misguidedly believe it does, which is why they go for comfort food, alcohol, and so on. They hope that by indulging in external pleasures, they will get to assuage their internal pain or unhappiness. It is true that such pleasures can seem to dull the pain and decrease depression, but such relief is very short term, while the pain and sadness lingers on.

3. **Internalized happiness (bliss):** This is when we feel happy and at peace with the world for no special reason. In fact, the normal state of the mind is often considered to be bliss by

some philosophers. I guess what they mean is that the tranquil mind is normally in a state of balance. When it gets off balance, then the thoughts and feelings start to race, and we go through ups (euphoria) and downs (depression, anger, and so on.)

Of the three, bliss seems a little difficult for me, so what I try to do is to focus on my internal happiness by choosing the thoughts that I hold in my mind. When I do that, I am able to enjoy external happiness too.

In closing I would like to leave you to ponder on the following quote about happiness by someone who lived more than two thousand years ago: "Happiness is the meaning and the purpose of life, the whole aim and end of human existence" (Aristotle).

Note #1: About the Mind

When I speak of mind, I am referring both to the intellectual part as well as the feeling or emotional parts. I am not separating the intellect as of the brain and feeling as of the heart. For all we know there could be certain parts of the brain that may be linked to feeling or emotion. It is merely standard convention to refer to the heart as the seat of feelings, but logically it cannot be true as proven in the case of heart transplants!

Recently I came across a news item about a sixty-five-year-old man who had a heart transplant more than fifteen years ago. In such a case obviously his feelings were not located in his heart, which had been removed. His feelings also could not be those of the donor who had already died.

Hence, I prefer to use the term *mind* in a broader sense without limiting it to the *brain* or the *heart* or the *gut* and so on. The mind (being a psychic component) is not limited to a specific physical part of the body. In fact, we may even consider it to be located throughout the human body, perhaps in every cell.

Note #2: About GOD versus God

Readers will notice that I use the term GOD as well as God in this book. There is a reason for this. When I speak of GOD, I am referring to the Creator, the Original Source *that existed long before humans were created and long before the world existed.*

Thus, *I believe in a GOD who made man and not in a God or gods made by man*!

To separate the original Creator or the Source from the man-made gods of mythology and theology, I use the term GOD as opposed to God.

See chapter 11 for a more complete discussion about this topic.

My Ode to Life

I believe that life is a miracle, perhaps the greatest miracle of all! The creation of the physical world (the galaxies with an infinite variety of suns, stars, and planets) pales in comparison with the creation of a human being.

For all their wonderful aspects, the planets and the suns are inanimate. They cannot recreate themselves or create anything new. The human being however is a living, breathing, thinking, and feeling being who is also a co-creator on her or his own terms.

He or she has been given the power to create things that are not found naturally in nature, such as music and art and books and buildings and cars and planes and computers and the Internet and so on. Hence, this creation of a human life has got to be the highest aspect of creation (in this dimension at least)!

Thus, on a personal level I believe that life is the greatest gift that we have been given. Without life there is nothing—no feelings, no experiences, no happiness, no sorrows, no purpose, no achievements, absolutely nothing!

CHAPTER 2

Why Do We Humans Seek Happiness?

Before I answer that question, let me first of all ask you this: What one thing does every one of us human beings want? What do we want so badly that we may prefer to die if we do not have it? What do we yearn for in this world? What are we human beings programmed to strive for?

We are not programmed merely to seek success, power, or even money as most of us believe. We all know examples of people with great power, wealth, and influence who still commit suicide. We also know of people at the other end of the spectrum (struggling with poverty, lack of power, lack of respect, and so on) who also try to kill themselves.

So what is the one thing in common that all these people from diverse backgrounds want so badly that they would prefer to die rather than go without?

In one word, the answer is happiness! Yes, happiness! All of us—from the poorest to the wealthiest, from the sinners to the saints, from the kings to the serfs—want happiness! And the fact is the Creator programmed us from birth only for happiness!

So the answer to the question posed at the beginning of this chapter is this: "We humans always seek happiness because we have been programmed to do so by the Creator."

How can I substantiate such a claim?

Just think about this: Has any one of us ever prayed for unhappiness? Have we prayed for less happiness as follows: "GOD, give me some misery. I am too happy in this world. I would like to be sad for a while."

I don't think so. I have yet to come across anyone who prayed for sorrow! We do not pray for sorrow because we are programmed by our Creator only for happiness and not for misery. (A more detailed discussion is given in chapter 12 under the title "We Are Programmed for Joy.")

Now you ask me, "If that is true, then why is there so much unhappiness in the world?" My answer is below.

Major Reason for Unhappiness

The major reason for unhappiness in this world is because we have not understood this primary requirement—that we are created in this wonderful world to be happy! In fact, we have been taught the exact opposite, and hence, we have not learned this truth.

Instead, right from childhood through our teens and even in adulthood, we have been taught the following:

- It is not right to be happy here and now. (This world is a place of punishment for the original sin of Adam and Eve, which all future generations have to suffer!)

- This world is a place for repayment of past bad karma—the best karma is not to be born and so on.

- We are told we may be happy only in the hereafter—since this world is one where we have to carry out our penances and carry out actions as prescribed by the religious authorities.

It is time to set the record straight. Let me say categorically once and for all, "GOD wants us to be happy! GOD wants us to be happy here on earth and in the hereafter."

The fact is that GOD so created this world and programmed our minds so that we can all achieve this state of happiness now! By doing so, we can also be happy in the hereafter.

It has never been an either-or situation as many would have us believe. We do not have to be miserable in this lifetime in order to be happy in the afterlife. You can have both—happiness here and now as well as in the hereafter.

How can I say this with such conviction? I have explained my thoughts and experiences about this at length, and these make up a major portion of this book.

Before some of you go and say, "It is selfish to think only of our own happiness," let me clarify a few things about what is real happiness.

Real happiness is all about empathy, desire, growth, achievement, and so on. It is all about positive emotions, feel-good emotions, and not feel-bad emotions! Real happiness is not selfish. We do not find real happiness at the expense of another. If some people think and act as though they can be happy only at another's expense, then they are only practicing pseudo happiness as I explain in a later chapter.

Real happiness is expansive, not contracting; it is inclusive and does not exclude. Happiness is not about greed, selfishness, lust, and so on, all of which is what I call pseudo happiness. So to avoid confusion, I shall instead call real happiness joy.

When we are truly happy or joyful, it is difficult to treat others badly. We feel generous, kind, and willing to overlook little slights and hurts. These same slights and injuries would make us rage if we were in an unhappy state. When we are really happy or joyful, we want others to share in the joy. Hence, we speak in a gentler tone. We are more forgiving and slow to anger. Thus, seeking to be really happy or joyful is not selfish.

Realize that being joyful is our birthright! In fact, being happy ranks even higher than self-preservation on the list of priorities of humans. That is why so many take their own lives. They feel that if they are going to be without happiness, then there is no point in living.

Now if happiness is so vital and we have been programmed to be happy, why do humans find it so hard to be happy and seem to be miserable most of the time? Because we humans have the wrong beliefs about happiness, about GOD, about the nature of the world, and about the nature of the mind!

If we only understood what happiness truly was and we knew the nature of the world and the laws of the mind, then we would be able to create the happy life we were programmed to live. We can choose to create our own desired reality rather than just accept or endure a miserable, unfulfilled life.

Let me illustrate a point about life with a small anecdote. Thomas Alva Edison (the great inventor of the electric bulb, gramophone, cinema projector, and so on) was once asked by a lady, "What is electricity?"

Edison replied very simply, "Madam, electricity is. Just use it!"

How wise Edison was. Even till today no one fully understands the actual nature of electricity, but we know enough to be able to control it and use it to our advantage.

Similarly people seem to be obsessed with the following question: "What is life?"

They spend so much time and energy in trying to answer that difficult (perhaps unanswerable) question! Thousands of books are written about it, and hundreds of ideas (some mere fantasies) are propounded. But none of them ever answers that question satisfactorily simply because we humans are not designed to answer such questions. We are only designed to live—to grow, co-create, and evolve.

Furthermore, it is not really necessary to know what life is in order to live a great, fulfilling, joyful life. All that is needed is to know **how** to live a happy life.

To those obsessed with this question, I would like to offer the same sage advice given by Edison. "Life is. Just live it to the best of your talents and ability!"

Take for example driving a car. To drive a car, you do not have to know who invented the car or about the Otto cycle or the limited slip differential or whether you have radial tires or antilock braking or any of the technical wizardry behind it. A book on the 'History of the Automobile' is of no help if you just want to learn how to drive a car!

To learn how to drive the car you need to learn only a few simple things. Just learn how to use the accelerator, the brake, the steering wheel, and so on, and soon you are flying down the highways. Learning the highway code also helps!

Similarly in order to live a joyful life, we only need to focus on living a great life now in this lifetime. We do not need to know who created the world and why. We also do not need to know about our previous lives. Neither do we need to know about the afterlife.

Yet that is what we have been constantly taught to obsess over; hence, we are unable to live happily in the present. Obsessing over unanswerable questions about GOD, past lives, and the afterlife is futile, but religions seem to have made a vocation of it.

To live a joyful life in this lifetime, we just have to ask, "How can we live a joyful life in the present?" All we need is to learn a few simple rules of happy living in order to live a great, wonderful life.

After years and years of study, frustration, confusion, and struggling to overcome many adopted beliefs and superstitions, I have finally formulated my own system of beliefs, which shows me how to be happy every day amid all the challenges of daily life.

This system of mine (which I call Joycentrix System) provides the keys to happiness and covers five cardinal beliefs.

1. Our beliefs about the Creator
2. Our beliefs about the world and reality
3. Our beliefs about creation, co-creation, and evolution
4. Our beliefs about the mind and how it works
5. Our beliefs about happiness

The main purpose of this book is to help people realize that happiness is a choice that each one of us can make. In closing this chapter, I would like you to ponder once again the same quote that I gave earlier and decide whether it feels true to you or not. Aristotle said, "Happiness is the meaning and the purpose of life, the whole aim and end of human existence."

So what do you think? Are we born into this world to live a joyful life or to suffer endless misery?

Assignment: Always Be Aware of Your Feelings and Your Thoughts at Any Particular Time!

For this assignment, just practice being aware of what you are feeling at any one time and check to see what thoughts are associated with that particular feeling.

- When you feel happy, what thoughts are in your mind?
- When you feel depressed, what thoughts are you holding on to?
- When you feel enthusiastic, what thoughts are you having in your mind?
- When you feel anxious and fearful, what thoughts are you holding on to?

Record these thoughts and their associated feelings down in a notebook. This exercise will help you to realize that it is the thoughts that you hold in your mind that give rise to your feelings of happiness or fear or misery or anger and so on.

PART 2

❖ The Power of Belief

❖ The Three Major Types of Beliefs

❖ Wrong Beliefs That Cause Unhappiness

❖ Misconceptions about Happiness

CHAPTER 3

The Power of Belief

First of all, some readers may be wondering why a chapter on belief should be included in a book on happy living. Well, the simple answer is because it is our beliefs that create our reality.

Our beliefs are built up over the years by the teachings of our parents, elders, our teachers, by age-old superstitions, by peers and friends, by books, and the public media. After a time each one of us forms our own sets of beliefs, and it is these sets of beliefs that control the way we live our lives.

In fact, we could say that each one of us is living in our own private world created by our own set of beliefs. For example, without being at all egotistic, I could say that I am living in "the world according to Gopi." So could each one of you! Just replace the word Gopi in the above phrase with your own name, and you have the truth about your own world and your own reality.

This is a fundamental truth: Each one of us lives in his/her own world according to the beliefs each holds about life!

Let's take some extreme cases to prove this point.

- The beliefs of a gangster are totally different from those of a philanthropist. Hence, you have to admit their worlds too are totally different!

- The beliefs of a nun are very different from those of a hooker. Hence, their worlds are very different, even if both live in the same city.

- The lives led by Einstein, Hitler, Gandhi, Edison, and Lincoln were each very different according to each one's beliefs.

- This is true even of members of the same family. The father's world is totally different from that of the mother's as is that of each child. Although they may live in the same house, each person's daily duties, their thoughts, actions, and responses are totally different—right from the time they wake up to the time they go to sleep. Even in sleep they have different dreams!

Thus, instead of saying, "The world according to me," you could just as well say, "My present beliefs about life and the universe that create my present reality!"

Therefore, it should come as no surprise that belief has a lot of power to keep us living happy or remaining miserable. In order to illustrate just how powerful beliefs can be to an individual, I would like to relate three stories about the power that resides in belief.

Stories about the Power in Belief

The first two intriguing stories are about miraculous healings. The first one is from Wallace D. Wattles, the author of the famous trilogy *Science of Being Well*, *Science of Being Great*, and *Science of Getting Rich* which were published about a hundred years ago.

His major principle in the *Science of Being Well* is this: "All those sick, who have been healed, by whatever system, became healed because of their own inner thoughts and beliefs—by thinking in a certain way."

1. **Healing Bones of a Saint:** It was said that several centuries ago the bones of a saint kept in one of the monasteries were working miracles of healing. On certain days in the year the bones were brought out and put on show. The public, which was suffering from illnesses and diseases, was allowed to touch the relics, and many who did so had a healing.

    One day on the eve of one of these appointed days for public display, they found out that some vandal had removed the wonder working bones. The monks were worried because the next morning there would be the usual crowds of people coming to be healed.

    They decided to hush up the matter (hoping to find and recover the relics soon) and replaced the lost bones with those of a criminal who had been buried at the churchyard years ago. They also planned to make up some excuse when the bones did not heal the masses.

    However, to their shock, the healings went on as normal—the bones of the criminal seemed to be just as effective at healing as those of the saint! One of the monks wrote a report of the occurrence and said, "The healing power had always been in the people themselves and not in the bones. What had brought the power out were the individual's own beliefs."

The second story of miraculous healing is from a book titled *Power of the Subconscious Mind* by Dr. Joseph Murphy, which I happened to read more than thirty years ago. I don't have a copy of the book with me now, so I'm just relating what I remember reading so many years ago.

2. **A White Lie Causes Miraculous Healing:** A young man had just gone on a tour of the holy sites in Jerusalem and the region. His father was critically ill with advanced tuberculosis (TB) and was said to have only a few months left to live.

   The son was devoted to his father and did not want to see him suffer the agonies of the disease. So he came up with a plan. He found a small piece of wood and set it in a nice metal frame and told his father, "I managed to buy this valuable relic when I was on tour in Jerusalem. The wood is a piece of the original cross on which Jesus was crucified. It is said that if you keep it with you, it can heal your illness."

   The father, who was a staunch believer in Christ, immediately grabbed the wood piece and held it to his chest reverently and was never without it. The strange thing is that he was cured of his TB, and instead of dying within a few months, he lived in good health for another eighteen years! Of course the son never told him the truth about the relic. If he had, the father might have suffered a relapse!

The third story I wish to relate is an ancient story in the Hindu classic Mahabharata that tells of a very inspiring incident that further illustrates the point that "the power of a belief is in the belief itself and not in the object of the belief!"

3. **The Story of Ekalavya:** Ekalavya was a poor woodcutter's son who lived in the forest and who had a great dream. He wanted to become expert in the art of using a bow and arrows. He wanted to be as great an archer as Arjuna (one of the Pandava princes who are the protagonists of the Mahabharata epic).

   So he went to see Drona (Arjuna's martial arts teacher or guru) and asked to be his disciple. Drona absolutely refused and arrogantly sent him off, saying that he would only teach martial arts to princes and not to a woodcutter.

   But this did not cause Ekalavya to despair. Instead he went back to his home in the forest and set about making a clay figure of Drona. Every day he would ask the blessings of his guru (the clay figure), believing that it was truly Drona in spirit. Then he would set about practicing his archery until he became really good at it.

   Several months later a team of hunters from the Pandava palace happened to go into this forest. The hunting dogs went on ahead, barking and making a ruckus. All of a sudden these dogs became quiet and came whimpering back to the hunters.

   They noticed that the dogs had their mouths sewn up. They were shocked and went to see who had had the courage to do that to the palace dogs. They found Ekalavya sitting in meditation. He had shut the dogs up with his mystical power of archery because they had disturbed his meditation. This made the hunters from the palace angry, and they attacked him. But he repelled them all easily with his wizardry at archery!

The hunters ran back to the palace and reported to Drona that there was someone in the forest who was an equal to Arjuna in archery. Drona rushed to the forest to check it out.

Immediately on seeing his spiritual guru, Ekalavya prostrated himself before him. Drona studied the situation, and because he did not want any woodcutter to be better than his pet student, Arjuna, he did an unthinkable thing.

He asked Ekalavya, "Do you really consider me your guru?"

Ekalavya replied, "Of course, you are my guru. It is only after getting blessings from you every day that I start my archery practices."

Then Drona said, "If what you say is true that I am indeed your guru, don't you owe me a guru 'dakshina' (a gift from the student for the guru)?"

Ekalavya replied, "Of course. What is it you want from me?"

Drona replied, "Would you give me your right thumb?" Immediately Ekalavya cut off his right thumb and gave it to Drona as a gift!

Drona had hoped that by losing his right thumb, Ekalavya would never be able to take up archery again. But Ekalavya never gave up, and soon he was as great an archer with his left hand as he had been before with his right!

This was one of the most inspiring stories I had heard when I was young—that one can achieve his dream if he truly believes in his own ability and perseveres in his attempts to achieve it! However, it also made me angry that a so-called guru (wise teacher) could be so self-serving and cruel!

That is also when I realized that the power of a belief is not in the object of the belief but in the belief itself! The object of Ekalavya's belief (Drona) may not have been worthy of his belief, but the power in Ekalavya's belief helped him to achieve his dream!

What I got from this story as well as the other two stories is the lesson that it is the power in our own beliefs that enable us to achieve great things or even healings. The power is not in the objects of that belief.

For example, in the last story, Drona was hardly deserving of the reverence he was given as a guru or great teacher. Similarly the bones of the criminal were not endowed with great powers of healing, and the saint's were not either. Also it was the son's blatant white lie that allowed his father to be cured and live to a ripe old age.

We have all heard of miraculous healing taking place in all places of worship to people of all faiths and religions. We have also heard of the term placebo in the medical field, where a sugar pill caused a miraculous recovery just because the patient had been told (and believed) that the pill was the latest discovery to cure his illness.

In all of these instances it was not the place or the object of their belief that restored the patients to health. It was their own unshakeable faith that they would be cured, which activated their own inner healing power. The only difference was in the manner in which their healing power was activated.

The truth is that there is only one healing force, which runs through each and every human being, and it can be activated by that person's belief. Each individual may use different means to activate this healing power within. Some visit holy places. Some make vows of fasting. Some abuse their bodies by fire-walking, pricking themselves with needles, and so on. However, all these methods can only work if and when they activate the healing power that is already present within each person.

You should note that nowadays many people have realized that they do not have to torture themselves or abuse their bodies in order to get a miraculous healing. They can use natural techniques like Reiki, Chi Kung, deep meditation, quantum touch, energy work, and so on—all of which are based on this principle that healing power is within everyone.

Even the medical doctors agree that they can only help nature; the actual curing is done by the patient's own inbuilt healing force. Just think of how a cut heals. We apply some antiseptic to keep away infection, and the body causes the cells to bind together, create a scar, and complete the healing.

I think belief works a little like the force of gravity. Gravity works equally on everything and everyone. It does not care if you a hero or you are a villain. It does not even matter if you believe gravity exists or not! It will not fail to act on anyone and anything.

Similarly the power in belief is neutral. It works for both good and bad beliefs. If you believe good things will happen, you attract good things, and if you believe that misery is your due, then you attract misery.

Belief works equally for wrong or detrimental beliefs as well as for beneficial beliefs. Belief has the power to motivate you to do things as well as the power to stop you from doing things. More than this, your subconscious (or unconscious) beliefs have the power to sabotage your best intentions.

Since there is so much power in belief, it is vital that we recognize just what beliefs we subscribe to at present because these beliefs are what create the reality we are experiencing now.

It is necessary to analyze our every belief and see which ones can give us joy and which ones cause us sorrow and misery. Once we see exactly how certain beliefs of ours are causing us problems, then it is only sensible to change them. As stated in the next chapter, all beliefs evolve when new truths are presented.

From the above stories we know just how much power there is in belief; to heal as well as help a person achieve his or her goal. However, the above examples only refer to one type of belief that gives positive results. I call these *intuitive beliefs*. There are a couple of other types of beliefs that I call *acquired beliefs* and *adopted beliefs*.

These beliefs as well as the positive and negative aspects (namely the beneficial or harmful aspects) of each are discussed in the next chapter.

CHAPTER 4

The Three Major Types of Beliefs

I ended the last chapter by stating that there are three major types of beliefs, namely acquired beliefs, intuitive beliefs, and adopted beliefs. These will be discussed in detail below.

Acquired Beliefs

Acquired beliefs are a common form of beliefs that are acquired by observation, experiment, and rational thinking. Acquired beliefs are very important in our daily lives. There are thousands of acquired beliefs. However, the few examples given below will clarify what I mean by acquired beliefs.

> **Seed Planted in the Ground:** You observe that a seed planted in the earth will grow into a plant after its own kind. If you plant an apple seed, you observe that it will grow in time into an apple tree, provided you give it water and nutrition and sunlight. If you

plant an orange seed, you will observe it grows into an orange tree. When you observe such a phenomenon repeatedly, you accept the belief that any seed planted in the ground will grow into a tree after its own kind. This is a belief acquired through observation, experimentation, and repetition.

Light Switch: Let us say that you come from the jungle and that you have never experienced electric light. You come across an electric light switch, and after several repetitions, you realize that each time you click it in one direction a light comes on and that when you click it in the opposite direction, the light goes off. Thereafter, you acquire a belief about the light switch and are able to turn it on or off as required.

Now if one day you switch it on and nothing happens, you will be at a loss to know what happened. You may repeat the process a few times and then give up.

However, with more information (such as the lamp bulb may be faulty, the switch itself may have loose contacts, or the power supply may have failed); your belief in the use of the light switch **evolves** by new knowledge, observation, experimentation, and repetition.

Sunrise: Having seen the sun rise up every morning day after day without fail, you believe that the sun will rise again on the morrow. You take it for granted. You have so much faith in this that you never pray at night, "God, please make sure the sun shines tomorrow." You are absolutely confident that it will shine tomorrow—even if you yourself do not wake up!

You need acquired beliefs to live normally in this world. For example, when you drive in the United States or Europe, you expect that all drivers will drive on the right, and you drive accordingly so that you are not involved in an accident. However, if you are in United Kingdom, India, or Australia, you have to believe that all drivers will drive on the left and thus adjust your driving (and even crossing the road on foot) accordingly or the results may be calamitous.

Acquired beliefs do evolve. Beliefs are not set in stone. They evolve and rightly so. Our beliefs change when more information is available than we could previously access. At one time we all believed in a flat earth. Now with new information we believe in a round earth. Similarly all our beliefs can and will evolve over time as we get more information and more proof.

Acquired beliefs are the basis of scientific and mathematical studies. By observation of some phenomena, we come up first with a hypothesis. Then we experiment and observe the results. We repeat the experiments under controlled conditions and study the results to come up with a scientific belief and call it a law.

These scientific laws (such as Newton's laws of motion) are then accepted as true until new information turns up which causes us to question them, and then we formulate new hypotheses, experiment again, and observe the results. And so the cycle continues. Thus, acquired beliefs are constantly evolving with time as new information and new observations and anomalous behavior that goes against the beliefs are observed.

Therefore, when our observation shows that the results of certain acquired beliefs are not in line with what is expected, we have to rethink and change our beliefs accordingly.

In the case of happy living principles, clinging on to the same old traditional beliefs (even in the light of new information) is counterproductive to happy results. Our beliefs must evolve to accommodate observed reality.

Intuitive Beliefs

Intuitive Beliefs are those beliefs that you somehow know to be true without any external proof or even observation. For example, Edison believed he could make a light bulb work despite repeated failures or proof to the contrary. All scientists, inventors, architects, chemists, entrepreneurs, and others have this intuitive belief that any particular thing they have imagined or visualized can be made to come true.

World-class athletes also follow their intuitive beliefs to achieve greatness and fame. We are all familiar with the story of Mohamed Ali (formerly Cassius Clay), who claimed, "I am the greatest," and proved it in the world of boxing. How could a novice boxer knock out the proven champion, Sonny Liston, and get the Olympic gold at the age of nineteen? Only because he had complete confidence in his intuitive belief that he would be the greatest boxer.

However, this does not mean that intuitive beliefs are restricted only to world-class athletes, inventors, scientists, or writers alone. Ordinary people, too, can do extraordinary things when directed by their own intuitive beliefs.

One of the best examples of intuitive beliefs can be seen in babies. *A baby does not need to observe another baby in order to learn to turn over or crawl or walk and then to run.* It does these things intuitively and instinctively. Even though it fails often when first trying to stand and then walk, the baby has an inner knowing that makes it continue to keep trying until it succeeds.

So an intuitive belief is definitely not an acquired belief. It does not come about through observation and study or rational thinking but purely from within the soul or spirit of the person. *This is what sets intuitive beliefs apart from other types of beliefs. They come not from external sources but from within.*

Some call it intuition. Others call it sixth sense. But whatever it is called, everyone has it. Some have developed this power, and others have neglected it; however, each one of us retains within us access to this awesome power from the primary Source or Creator. We will talk more of this power of intuition in the chapter on mind.

Personally I first learned about intuitive beliefs from small personal successes that could be considered almost trivial.

- **Story #1:** When I was in college, I had a good friend named Mike who was a great table-tennis (ping-pong) player. In fact, he was on the college team. One day he asked me, "Gopi, why don't you take up table tennis? It is a good game for you."

  I replied, "Ping-Pong looks like a silly game to me—you great big adults hitting a small, almost weightless ball. Tennis may be interesting, but ping-pong is just plain silly!"

  Mike was understandably miffed with my comments and said, "I think you are saying that only because you will never be able to play it. I dare you to take up ping-pong as a challenge, but I know that even after three months I will still beat you under ten points!"

Well, I really thought that it was an easy game and accepted his challenge. However, when I began to play, I found that I could not keep the ball on the table whether it was on serve or on return. The ball kept shooting off in all directions, and I was more tired picking up the ball than in playing the game.

I realized then that it was much more difficult than I had first thought. In fact, as far as the challenge was concerned, everything was stacked against me. I had never before held a ping-pong paddle, while Mike had been playing all through his school days and was now on the college team. All my friends told me to back out from the challenge.

However, I didn't feel like giving up. Something told me I could do it (intuitive belief), and I started to practice in earnest. Fortunately I found another friend who was a respectable player though not on the college team and who served as a good teacher. He patiently showed me how to serve, how to return, how to topspin and as well as how to underspin the ball; how to defend against an attacking shot with a defensive chop or a counterattack, and so on.

I practiced avidly every day while I focused on playing a winning game and never allowed doubtful thinking to interfere because I intuitively believed I could win the challenge.

At the end of one month Mike could not beat me "under ten points," and within three months, I was able to beat him occasionally. Personally it was an amazing achievement for me—developing from a complete novice at table tennis to becoming someone who was able to beat a college player who had played the game from childhood.

The above may seem to be a trite or trivial example, but it does illustrate the power of intuitive beliefs to make a person do seemingly impossible things. It does not matter if an intuitive belief is used for purely personal achievements (like a baby walking or a person going from rags to riches) or for something that causes a huge impact on humanity and life (like the invention of motor vehicles or computers). The power in intuitive belief is the same, and it is amazing.

An intuitive belief acted upon with confidence is what fuels co-creation, whereby we can help in the evolution of the world. This aspect of creation is discussed in a later chapter on creation and co-creation.

Adopted Beliefs

Adopted beliefs are the most common types of beliefs prevalent in this world. Each one of us has adopted hundreds if not thousands of beliefs in our lifetimes—many of these in our childhood.

During childhood our minds are not yet developed enough to question our parents or our teachers. We accept and adopt their beliefs unquestioningly because of our love, respect, and reverence for them. Whether the beliefs are true or beneficial or detrimental to us does not matter. We adopt their beliefs blindly and with full trust.

This innocent, trusting behavior of children has been used to great effect by religious teachers and charismatic leaders to manipulate their minds for centuries. When these adopted beliefs are created in childhood and made habitual by continued repetitions, even when the children grow up to become adults, they dare not question these beliefs. There is a saying in Tamil that translates to state, "Habits learned in the cradle will last right up to the grave!"

This is proven time and again in our own lives. The child becomes an adult and then becomes a parent who teaches these same self-defeating adopted beliefs to his or her own children, and so the cycle of ignorance continues.

We neglect our GOD-given power of reason and rational thinking because we are afraid to use critical thinking when it goes against our adopted and habitual beliefs. We prefer to avoid rocking the boat and say things like the following:

- "If it is good enough for my parents and grandparents, it is good enough for me."
- "So many million persons will not be following these beliefs if it were not true."
- "Who am I to question the masters?"

I shall be discussing this in more detail in a later chapter.

Superstitions are adopted beliefs that defy logic and reason. The difference between superstition and an adopted belief is that in the case of superstition we adopt the beliefs of others whom we don't necessarily revere or respect. This is the category where people believe things merely on hearsay just because of a general fear of the unknown. They believe that the world is unfriendly to them. Hence, they tend to desperately clutch at straws as a solution. They say silly outlandish things like these statements:

- "Throw salt over your shoulder for good luck."
- "Don't start your journey if a black cat crosses your path."
- "Avert bad luck by doing this or that." (You can insert anything totally illogical and irrelevant that you may have heard.)

Superstitions do not benefit us but can even cause problems. For example, belief in voodoo can cause one to suffer pain and disease because it works like placebo in reverse. You have so much fear or faith in the evil that is predicted that your body begins to create the circumstances believed in.

This is not fantasy. It is fact. *When you believe strongly that your body is going to be affected by something, you cause the very thing to appear in your body—whether it is encouraging healing or creating illness.*

In the Philippines during every Lent festival we come across some people whose hands and feet show stigmata, which duplicate the same wounds on Christ's hands and feet when he was crucified. Stigmata seem to arise spontaneously and heal by themselves too. It is believed that stigmata arise because the devotee's mind is so focused on the sufferings of Jesus (while in deep meditation) that his or her mind literally causes the skin to bleed and wounds to appear. There is also the probability that the person might have self-inflicted these wounds but his mind forgets (or represses) the event to preserve his belief. Even so the mind is the master and belief is the principle at work here.

In Malaysia at Batu Caves during the world-renowned Thaipusam Festival, dozens of devotees fast for several days, and on the festival day they pierce their tongue and cheeks with needles and use hooks to hang objects on their bodies. But they don't suffer any pain, and their wounds heal miraculously.

During some Chinese festivals you will find many people fire-walking on hot coals without any burn marks on their feet. Indians, too, have their own fire-walking ceremonies. They all believe that it is their faith in their god that enables them to do this.

How then do we explain the fact that some attendees at a Tony Robbins weekend seminar are also able to walk over hot coals without any harm? In fact, fire-walking is an item held on the last day prior to graduating from the seminar.

We also find that people are able to perform amazing feats with their bodies when under hypnosis. Hypnotic anesthesia has been used sometimes in dental surgery. Hypnosis has been used to reduce bleeding and speed up blood clotting, especially with hemophilic patients. Hemophilia is a rare genetic disorder that prevents the blood from clotting properly.

Similarly incredible feats are performed by kung fu and chi kung masters, such as bending an iron bar with the throat, holding a piece of blistering hot lead (that can burn right through a cardboard box) on the tongue, and many other seemingly impossible things.

In all these cases it is my contention that it is the power in the belief itself (whether it is intuitive belief, adopted belief, acquired belief, or even superstition) that causes the body to exhibit such marvels.

Summary

In this chapter we talked about the three major types of beliefs, namely acquired beliefs (brought about by observation, experiment, and repetition), intuitive beliefs (an inner knowing not based on external reality), and adopted beliefs (those we adopt blindly from the people we revere and respect). We also talked of superstition, which is an adopted belief based on hearsay and adopted out of fear of the unknown.

In the next chapter we will talk about specific adopted beliefs that are detrimental to our quest for happiness, how they came about, and what to do to change them when our observation shows that the results are not what we want.

In the case of happy living principles, clinging to the same old beliefs (even in the light of new information) is counterproductive to happy results. Our beliefs must evolve to accommodate observed reality.

Assignment

List some of the adopted beliefs you hold on to at present that you feel are not benefiting of you as far as your quest for happiness is concerned. In other words just write down a list of some beliefs you may have that are causing you unhappiness. For example, these could include the following:

- "This world is one of suffering."
- "We are all sinners and hence need to suffer."
- "Money is the root of all evil."

It will be beneficial for you to do this before you read the next chapter, which is all about wrong beliefs that cause unhappiness.

CHAPTER 5

Wrong Beliefs That Cause Unhappiness

As I explained in a previous chapter, it is our adopted beliefs that cause us the most unhappiness. Many of these beliefs come in the form of wise sayings or proverbs or statements that have been drummed into our heads and our hearts and accepted by almost everyone as true.

There are thousands of such beliefs that are operating at a subconscious level and causing us untold misery without us even realizing it. What I hope to do in this chapter is to bring to our conscious attention just a few of these age-old myths and shine the light of reason on them. By doing so I hope readers will become aware of some of the beliefs that could be causing problems for them.

I shall start with one statement that takes the cake for being a major cause for our collective unhappiness as human beings. If I were to say, "Man proposes—" I am quite sure you would automatically complete the phrase with this: "God disposes!" That is how much we believe in that proverb. But what does this really mean?

Man Proposes; God Disposes!

What a depressing thought? If we really believe this, then we are doomed to lifelong unhappiness because we would be fighting a losing battle. How can we puny humans fight against the might of God? No wonder we feel miserable. Even before we start, we are assured of failure.

It is because we have this belief that so many of us feel the need to start off any new project with prayers, hoping to appease God and get his blessings.

But really, how can we ever think that the Creator, who is said to be omnipotent (all-powerful) and omniscient (all-knowing), and ever-loving (all-compassionate), is out to prevent us from achieving what we want? How absurd!

Does it make sense to think that GOD is just waiting to spoil all our well-laid plans? Why would our creator, who has created a wonderful world for us to live in, to experience, to enjoy, and to develop our innate potential to the fullest, then do an about-turn to try to stop us from achieving our dreams or goals?

It is just plain silly! If GOD is considered a father figure, as most of us are repeatedly taught by our religions, then how can GOD ever go against our dreams and goals? Would any of you as a father or mother ever try to put obstacles in the way of your children's achievement?

Of course not! You would do your best to ensure that your children get the best possible help in going after their dreams! So isn't it a grave injustice to consider GOD as acting against the wishes of his children, us humans?

NOTE: Of course some readers could argue that assigning human traits and behavior to GOD as being a parent is very limiting to a perfect, infinite being. A point well taken, but isn't this exactly what everyone is doing and have been doing for centuries when they talk of god's vengeance, of praying for blessings or praying to appease god, of sinning and punishment (hell), of virtue and reward (heaven) and so on? I am merely using the same analogies but thinking of GOD in a better, more loving, and more positive light.

Imagine how much happier we would be if we changed that saying to this: "Man proposes; GOD endorses!" This is the truth anyway. Just like any good parent, GOD is happy for us to achieve our dreams.

But unfortunately that is not how we have been brought up. We have instead been brought up to look at everything in as negative a manner as possible. Just think of the aphorisms that we have been fed with since childhood:

- *We are born into this world as punishment because of the sins of our forefathers.* All the great religions subscribe to this type of thinking. We were kicked out of heaven because of original sin. We are born into this world to suffer because of karma and so on. So instead of thinking of this life or this world as a wonderful gift, we think of it as a curse.

- *You can't have everything!* I guess even George Bernard Shaw, the great playwright (who wrote Pygmalion, which became the movie titled My Fair Lady), subscribed to this type of thinking. There is a well-known joke attributed to him, which goes as follows:

At a party in his honor a stunning blonde approaches G. B. Shaw and says, "Wouldn't it be wonderful if we got married and we had a child with your brains and my beauty?"

Shaw is supposed to have replied sarcastically, "Madam, what happens if the child is born with your brains and my beauty?"

First of all he, too, believed that "beauty and brains didn't go together" (even though that is not always true). Therefore, he assumed the beautiful blonde must be stupid just because she was good-looking! Secondly he forgot that even if the blonde were not brainy, there was still a fifty-fifty chance of her assumption coming true.

If even a great intellectual like George Bernard Shaw can succumb to such negative conditioning, what about normal everyday people like us? When we have been continually bombarded with such negatives, it is impossible to retain a positive attitude. How then can we be happy? Here are some more misery-making proverbs and familiar sayings that are quoted regularly:

- *There is many a slip between the cup and the lip!* Can you imagine just how negative that statement is? You have a cup of coffee in your hand, and you are looking forward to enjoying the drink. What the saying suggests is that the cup may not reach your lips. You may never get to drink the coffee! Similarly for your dreams and goals—so near yet so far!

- *If you laugh too much today, you will have to cry tomorrow!* My siblings and I had that drummed into our heads when we were kids so much so that we were afraid of being too happy. We always expected the worst.

- *Money is the root of all evil!* This one is classic and has caused more misery than any of the other 'wise' sayings. For centuries money has been abused, and it has been called every sort of bad name by all and sundry. The religions, the great gurus, why even the ordinary man in the street has something bad to say about money. Some say, "Money is the root of all evil." Others say, "Love of money is the root of all evil." Some curse the wealthy as being filthy rich, obscenely wealthy, and so on. Does money deserve such a bad name?

  Talking of evil let me give you some scary statistics. Did you know that 99.9 percent of all crimes in the world are committed by *sighted* people, by people who can see! Isn't that true? Have you heard of a blind snatch thief, blind armed robber, blind rapist, or blind assassin? Not really!

  Therefore, is it logical to say that eyesight is the root of all crime? Thus, to eradicate crime in the world, all we have to do is just blind everyone at birth! Isn't that an absurd conclusion? Eyesight is a wonderful blessing.

  Similarly money is a great blessing. What do we first look for when we hear of tsunamis, earthquakes, hurricanes, and other catastrophes? Donations! We look for money. If we want to take our kids to Disneyland, we need money. If we want to build hospitals, schools, and places of worship, we also need money. For heart surgery, for buying a Mercedes, for even a bottle of mineral water, we use money. The only thing free so far is air. So money ranks only second to air because we need money for everything else!

Now what exactly is money? Money is a wonderful invention made for our convenience. It is a means of exchange, a measure of value. Before money was invented, all transactions were done by bartering. Can you imagine having to barter with goods for everything we need?

Imagine going to a BMW showroom with a herd of cattle for barter! Whether we use money for doing wonderful things or for crime and war depends entirely on us, our thinking.

In conclusion, let me categorically state that money is blameless. Money is neutral. Money by itself cannot write a book or cook a dinner or grow a garden or start a war or build a hospital. Only people can!

Therefore, let us from today onward decide to stop using such negative terms regarding money and wealth as: filthy rich, obscenely wealthy, etc. Instead let us say blessedly rich or wonderfully wealthy.

- *Whatever can go wrong will go wrong (Murphy's Law).* This has got to take the prize as being absolutely the most ridiculous statement ever, what more to call it a law! Just think of all the millions of things that are going right each day. If we keep quoting this silly law then it is no wonder we always worry about the outcome of anything that we are really looking forward to achieving. Thus, we expect things to go wrong more often than expect things to go right.

Fortunately great inventors like Edison, Ford, Bell, and others never heard about this law. Otherwise we would not have electric light, the automobile, or the telephone! I am grateful that such enlightened people used an alternative law that says, "Whatever can go right will go right!" May I call this Gopi's Law?

• *You can't take it with you.* Who has not heard this admonition? People regularly tell us this when we attempt to acquire material riches for the enhancement of our family's lifestyle. Others who are too lazy or fearful of making an attempt to raise the standard of living for themselves and their families also regularly use this as an excuse for not doing anything!

If people tell me "You can't take it with you"; I answer, "Of course not! Why would I want to?"

If people really believed in this adage, then there would be no travel industry! When I travel to Venice and ride the gondola, can I take back the gondola? When I stay at a five-star hotel, can I take back the hotel? Of course, some of us may try to sneak out the cutlery or the monogrammed towels, but generally we don't expect to take back the superior bed or luxury bathtub.

When we study at a certain university campus, can we take back our room at the campus or the friends we make? Of course not!

And we don't want to!

But does that mean that we should avoid the experience altogether just because we can't take it with us? How ridiculous to even think that. But that is just what this superstition makes you do.

All we want to do (and can do) is take back the experience, the feelings, the joy, the excitement that we experienced when we were there!

Similarly for the material things in this wonderful GOD-created world, all these material things are here for us to enjoy, to use, to experience, to help in our growth while we are here—that is all.

To refuse to acquire and use whatever we can to enhance our happiness just because "we cannot take it with us" has got to be the ultimate in illogical thinking. It is also a false belief or superstition of the silliest sort.

• *This life is temporary, not permanent!* So what? Who wants this to be permanent? We can enjoy life in all its fullness only when it is transitory! GOD so designed this world that the transitory pleasures make life worth living. Nobody can enjoy anything continuously.

Take going to a play or the theater or to a great restaurant or playing tennis or even making love for example. Would you like to spend your whole life in the theater or at the restaurant or playing tennis or making love? Of course not! Each of those things you enjoy only when it is time-limited and not if you had to spend hours doing only that.

The great masters tell me that this life is transitory and impermanent. How wonderful? I don't want to be an immortal here on this earth. When I finish my experiences here on earth, I am happy to go to newer experiences in other dimensions just as the Creator has planned.

They also tell me that only my soul is permanent and immortal! How utterly fabulous? All the more reason to live a full, enriched, happy life here on earth before my soul takes flight. So now I can confidently look forward to life after death because I trust in the wisdom of GOD, and I know that everything is going to be for the best.

In this chapter we have looked at a few of the common aphorisms that have heavily influenced us since childhood. We have put them up to the light of reason and logic and hopefully come up with sensible alternatives. However, there are hundreds more such inane sayings that masquerade under the guise of wisdom.

Unfortunately this is the type of drivel we are fed mentally from childhood. No wonder most of us adults are screwed up in our thinking. And because our thinking is all messed up, our lives too are all messed up. How then can we be happy? No wonder most people feel that misery is the lot of human beings. But it is not and does not have to be.

Life is a wonderful gift and this world is a wonderful place for us to explore and express ourselves and fulfill our dreams and aspirations!

Assignment

By analyzing several of these well-known myths in this chapter, I hope I have pointed the way for readers to question other so-called wise sayings that they have repeatedly heard or will encounter.

For today's assignment, think of at least five popular sayings that you have been using in your daily conversation or reading.

Write these down and analyze them using your logic and reason. Decide if these adopted beliefs are helping you to be happy or otherwise.

If you find that the beliefs are counterproductive to your own happiness, just discard them from your vocabulary and create alternative beliefs that will help.

CHAPTER 6

Misconceptions about Happiness

Misconception #1: Happiness Is Out There to Be Pursued and Captured

Since time immemorial people have been pursuing happiness, but they don't seem to be any nearer to capturing it. This is because they have been misinformed and deluded for centuries.

For example, even the American Declaration of Independence contains these famous words: "We hold these truths to be self-evident, that all men are created equal, that they are endowed by their Creator with certain unalienable rights that among these are life, liberty, and the pursuit of happiness."

Because the words *the pursuit of happiness* have been uttered in the same breath as life and liberty, people accept the idea of pursuing happiness to be a self-evident truth too. And they assume it to be literally true. They expect happiness to be found somewhere external to themselves, but this is just not so.

Happiness is not out there to be pursued and captured. True happiness comes from within us and is to be created and experienced. It is by not understanding this that most people spend all their lives pursuing happiness and end up dying miserable.

If happiness is truly out there, then we should be able to name specific locations (such as certain countries or cities where happiness is rampant) and other locations where misery is the norm. Similarly we would find that only people living under certain circumstances (such as having material success and possessions) can be happy.

However, the truth is that people can be found to be happy in all countries and cities, in all kinds of dwellings, with or without luxury vehicles for transport. There are people who are happy while they are living in large cities and others who are happy living in farms or even in remote villages of the Arctic.

On the other side of the coin, there are people living in diverse locations and circumstances who are still unhappy. In fact, it is common to find people who may be living on the same street, yet one is happy while another is miserable. Thus, external circumstances are not the only criteria for real happiness or joy.

Granted that external circumstances can make one feel good temporarily, but such happiness is a merely a reaction to and depends on outside circumstances. Unfortunately most people think that this type of happiness is the only real happiness. That is why people are constantly engaged in the pursuit of happiness, expecting to catch up with happiness once they get something external. They often think the following:

- *If only I had more money, I would be happy.*
- *If only I could afford a Mercedes car, I would be happy.*
- *If only I could travel the world, then I would be happy.*
- *If only I had a better job, I would be happy.*
- *If only I had a nicer home, I would be happy.*
- *If only I had a more supportive family and friends, I would be happy.*

After much struggle many of them do achieve several of these external goals, but real happiness still eludes them. That is why so many financially and professionally successful people still feel unhappy and empty inside. They have not realized that real happiness and joy is found within.

This does not mean that we need to be poor to be happy as some teachers falsely infer. You can and should have external material goals, but you need to be already happy inside before you can truly enjoy your external successes. I cover this topic fully in a later chapter under "happiness enhancers."

> Once we realize that happiness is within each one of us and can be created purposely by us and made into a regular habit, we can make happy living a daily part of our lives!

The above sentence covers the essence of what I am sharing in this book. However, I know it is a great stretch for people to go from thinking, *Happiness is out there to be pursued and captured,* to thinking, *Happiness is within us to be created and experienced!*

Therefore, the primary motivation of this book is to facilitate this transition in thinking—gradually leading the readers a step at a time so that anyone can follow the logic as well as the practical application of the happy living principles and tips I am sharing.

You should note that the principles and tips that I share in this book are what I personally used (and still use) to change my decades of frustration and misery to one of daily happiness. Does that seem too good to be true? Why not just keep an open mind and follow along and then make your own decision. Accept it or reject it—that's your GOD-given choice—but at least hear me out first.

Misconception #2: Mistaking Pseudo Happiness for Real Happiness

The second grave misconception about happiness is in mistaking pseudo happiness for real happiness or joy. Many people believe that they can get happiness from the misery of others! This is what I term *pseudo happiness* or false happiness! Some other types of pseudo happiness are listed below:

- punishment and revenge (when we feel good because we are meting out justice)
- bullying and sadism (poor self-image that needs another to suffer for one to feel happy)
- verbal and physical abuse (another case of poor self-image with a need to feel superior in order to be happy)

But none of these offers any real happiness. Let us just think about this. How exactly do you feel in the following instances?

- when you are angry
- when you have hatred in your heart
- when you envy another
- when you think about injustice

In each of the above examples, the feeling you get is not one of happiness. We do not feel good when we are angry! We do not feel happy when we hate someone or something. We do not feel happy when we are envious. We do not feel happy when we think about injustice.

So why then do so many of us insist on venting our anger, taking revenge, and so on?

I think it is because what we feel is **relief** (such as when a thorn in our flesh is removed), which we mistake to be happiness! While relief is preferable to pain, it is still not real happiness.

Unfortunately this avoidance of pain and unhappiness is what many people assume to be happiness. Many of us resort to drinking, ritual worship, drugs, and so on to assuage the pain and misery we feel. This only gives temporary relief, helping us forget our misery for a time, but it is not real happiness. All of these (including singing hymns, drinking to forget, taking drugs, and so on) are merely methods to achieve pseudo happiness.

Real happiness, on the other hand, is not mere relief but actually feeling good! Real happiness is expansive and makes you feel loving and tolerant. It is inclusive and does not exclude others. In other words we cannot really be happy by making another miserable! Real happiness is not derived by avoiding unhappiness any more than we can heal heartbreak with comfort food or alcohol!

Since there is so much misunderstanding about real and pseudo happiness, we have decided to use the term *joy* for *real happiness* interchangeably for the purposes of this book.

Misconception #3: Believing that Only Certain People Are Destined for Happiness

This is another of those adopted beliefs that we accepted when we were children. The words such as *fated, destined, born-lucky*, etc. have been drilled into us so many times that we believe only some people deserve happiness and are destined to have it while the majority is doomed to misery.

This misconception is what keeps the class concept intact in this world. For example, consider the following:

- In India we have the caste system to segregate sections of society.
- In the United States we used to have the masters and slaves.
- In Europe we used to have royalty and the serfs.
- Everywhere in the world we have the upper class and the lower class, the rich and the poor.

However, if we believe that we have all been created by GOD with free will and the ability to choose our thoughts and our actions, then anyone can have happiness—provided that they use the power of their own mind to create synchronistic effects in the universe that will help them achieve their own happiness.

It is only *when people feel powerless that they resort to labeling others as inferior in order to think they themselves are superior.* If one truly believes in a benevolent Creator, one does not need the crutches of position, prestige, or power or need to label others as inferior in an attempt to attain happiness. Each one of us is endowed with the power of choice and the power of our mind to create our own happy life.

You should note that there is the exception of certain disabled persons who do not seem to have this power of choice and mind power. I cannot explain the reason for this or for the myriad unanswered questions about life, but I have ventured to discuss something similar in part 3 under the heading "Why Does GOD Allow Bad Things to Happen?"

However, if we believe that we are prevented from happiness by fate, karma, our status in society, and so on, we will sabotage ourselves at every opportunity and make that belief become reality.

*   *   *

The above are some of the major misconceptions about happiness that we subscribe to, which is why many of us find it hard to be happy.

If these are all misconceptions, what then is the truth about happiness? We discuss this in the chapter titled "The Truth about Happiness." But before we do that, let me introduce you to what I call the Joycentrix System.

This is my own system of beliefs (that I acquired after years and years of study, struggle, frustration, and overcoming many superstitions), which allows me to be happy every day amid all the challenges of daily life.

The Joycentrix System promotes confidence, peace of mind, and happiness rather than worry, fear, and unhappiness. It is described in the next part of the book.

PART 3

CHAPTER 7

The Joycentrix System

The Joycentrix System is the name I have given to the system of beliefs that I have acquired over the years, the system that enables me to be joyful in spite of negative circumstances. It also helps me to create better circumstances to enhance my happiness.

As explained in chapter 2, each one of us is programmed by the Creator to be joyful and to spread joy. The true inner motivation behind everything we do is really our desire for joy. Thus, if our thoughts, words, and deeds are aligned with being joyful and spreading joy, then our life is centered on joy. Hence, we have the term *Joycentrix*.

In an earlier chapter I spoke about the power in beliefs to create our reality. We know that wrong beliefs can cause unhappiness while the right beliefs can lead to happiness. The right beliefs to enable happiness and joy are contained within the five cardinal rules in the Joycentrix System.

Cardinal Rule #1: Belief in a Benevolent and Compassionate GOD, Not a Vengeful and Vindictive One

- *I believe that the Creator is kind, compassionate, and loving like a good parent!* In addition, I believe GOD is nonjudgmental and forgiving unlike most humans. Therefore, GOD is not a vindictive dictator who needs to be continually appeased with offerings and sacrifices! GOD always has our best interests at heart. Humans were not created to be mere pawns and puppets to be manipulated at the whims and fancies of God or gods (as the Greeks believed about Zeus, Hera, and so on). We humans have been created with free will and the power to co-create through the use of our minds.

- *I believe that the Creator is infinitely more intelligent and compassionate than we are!* Therefore, this world that GOD created must be the very best there could ever be—the ideal place for us to explore, to experience, and to express ourselves to the best of our talents and abilities at our present level of evolution! If we truly believe that the Creator is good and has our best interests at heart, we do not have to keep searching for a better world. If we thought otherwise, (namely that GOD does not want the best for us and is only keen on judging and punishing us), then life is really going to be torture. I find it contradictory (even paradoxical) when people say they revere the Creator but have no respect for GOD's creation, namely this world. They claim this world is illusion (i.e., unimportant) or a place of punishment where people are born to suffer.

Cardinal Rule #2: Knowing the True Nature of the World.

- *This world is a supportive place that enables humans to evolve, not a place of punishment or a penitentiary.* I believe that this world is like a school or university! It is not a prison where we are forced to suffer as punishment for our past sins. Instead, the world is a wonderful place of education and development with all the facilities (such as libraries, labs, playing fields, swimming pools, etc.) for us to learn, grow, make friends, and have fun.

- *I believe that living in this world is like being in a particular class or form.* If I do well in say form one, then I will be promoted to form two automatically. If, on the other hand, I do badly in this class, I may have to come back to repeat the class! And remember that the universe has infinite time. It can allow me to repeat the same class a hundred or a thousand times. (This we call reincarnation or living several lifetimes.)

- *So I believe that my only priority in life is to live well.* If I lead a great, fulfilled life here, I do not have to worry about the afterlife or fear it! I will be promoted to the next dimension in good time, and that place, too, will be good!

Cardinal Rule #3: Knowing the Nature of the Mind and How We Can Use Our Minds to Create Our Own Happiness

- *I believe that our minds have the power to create our reality!* As stated earlier, our beliefs create our reality. And our minds can be used to formulate our beliefs. Hence, our minds can create our individual reality. When I speak of reality I am not talking about imagined reality but actual material circumstances. We can change our circumstances through the use of powers latent in our minds. Rather than just accepting any mediocre life, we have the power to design our own happy, successful lives! This is discussed later under happiness enhancers.

- *I believe that the mind is much more than the brain!* Awareness is much more than the five senses or the intellect. The mind includes feelings and emotion. Feelings are unseen, and emotions are not measurable; however, no one can deny they do exist.

- *I believe that the powers of the mind are tremendous!* In fact, we have barely scratched the surface with all our studies in psychiatry and psychology and medicine. We are only just beginning to understand the true awesome power of our minds.

- *I believe that there are certain unalterable laws of the mind!* There is one particular law of mind that works for everyone—*what we focus our thoughts on and believe in wholeheartedly is what we create in our reality!*

It works for bad as well as good. If we focus constantly on sickness (talk about it, read about it, think about it), we will get sick! If we constantly focus on health, refusing to dwell on opposing thoughts, then we can realize health.

If we focus with confidence on achieving our goal without allowing any doubtful thoughts, then we will achieve our goal! Similarly if we focus our awareness and our thoughts on happiness and joy, then this is what we achieve.

Cardinal Rule #4: Knowing the Truth about Evolution and Co-creation

- *I believe that evolution is a necessary part of creation!* Believing in evolution does not mean that we have to stop believing in GOD as many people seem to think. The way I see it, there is no contradiction here. Evolution is an integral part of creation, not separate from it. Every living thing is programmed to grow and evolve. In addition, humans have the choice of how they grow and to what heights. When individuals use this power of choice, the world evolves—generally for the better and sometimes for the worse—but we still retain the power to check any decline.

- *I believe that creation is ongoing and that we are co-creators!* Creation is ongoing. It has not ended. GOD has not gone to sleep after seven days. While GOD carries on the macro creation and micro creation, we humans have been tasked with co-creation (the managing of this university called Earth) and given the powers necessary to co-create and help evolution on this planet.

Cardinal Rule #5: Knowing the Truth about Happiness

- *I believe that happiness is a choice!* So is sorrow. So is anger. So is love. What we decide to focus on in our minds is what we end up feeling and experiencing.

- *I believe that if we choose love, we will be happiest!* I am talking of unconditional love here, not reciprocal love. The second type of love (as extolled in the romances of Mills & Boon) can give happiness but can also give rise to misery if it is not reciprocated! However, unconditional love (that which we feel when we look at an infant, a pet, and so on) is not based on reciprocation. We do not expect the infant to smile for us or dance for us to be worthy of our love. We just love with no expectation of reward!

- *I believe that pleasure (short-term happiness) is of the senses while joy and peace of mind (long-term happiness) is based on the thoughts we cultivate in our mind!* We know full well that our senses can give us pleasure immediately without any thinking being involved. Hearing a haunting melody, biting into a juicy, ripe red apple, seeing a beautiful sunset, the aroma of a special perfume, the hug of a loved one—all these can instantly make us feel happy!

  But it is our attitude that gives long-term happiness or peace of mind. For example, imagine you have just received news of the death of a close family member. Would you then be able to find pleasure in eating the fruit? Or in seeing the sunset? Or in hearing the melody? No! Because pleasure is of the senses, but real happiness (joy) is of the mind!

These are the basic beliefs that make up the Joycentrix System at this present time! Of course, some of these beliefs may evolve over time with new knowledge and new experiences, but generally I find these beliefs make happy living a daily reality for me.

I will be discussing each of these in detail below because each belief uncovers several different principles and laws of the universe.

CHAPTER 8

Joycentrix Rule #1: Belief in a Benevolent GOD

O ne of the fundamental principles of happy living is our concept of GOD (the Creator or the Source). Our belief about the Creator makes it either easy to be happy or easy to be miserable!

Almost everyone claims to believe in God. My question for you is this: Just what kind of GOD do you believe in? Do you believe in a GOD who is benign and compassionate or one who is vengeful and judgmental? Is GOD a tyrant or dictator?

If you subscribe to the idea that GOD is an intractable dictator who swears, "Vengeance is mine," who is always looking over your shoulder to check on all the mistakes and sins that you commit (even in your thoughts), then it is very difficult to live a happy life!

Imagine your boss was peeking at your work (all the time), looking for faults, slipups, and so on. Wouldn't it be torture working at such an office?

Similarly if you believed that GOD was forever watching you, judging you, waiting to punish or reward you, wouldn't it put too much stress on you to live a happy life? In fact, it would be like living in a country ruled by a dictator—a dictator who would punish not only you but everyone in your family if you disobeyed him. It would be a veritable hell on earth to live in such a country!

So the question is this: Is GOD a dictator?

I answer with a vehement no! Unfortunately our great religions say otherwise. Many Christian believers say that we should fear God, that God is vengeful, that we should beware of Judgment Day, and so on. They say that we would all have been in paradise if only Adam had not eaten of the Tree of Knowledge, which was forbidden.

When I first heard this story as a primary school pupil in a Christian mission school, I was quite surprised and asked the teacher, "Why would GOD forbid anyone to eat of the Tree of Knowledge? Is knowledge such a bad thing? If knowledge is bad, why are we told to attend school?" The teacher told me to stop asking such questions and just accept what was told.

They also taught me that Adam and Eve were banned from paradise to suffer on earth because our ancestors disobeyed GOD and ate of the forbidden fruit. Not only that, but all subsequent generations had to suffer too (because of the original sin of Adam and Eve)!

Can GOD be that vindictive? Even we humans (except for some dictators) show more mercy and compassion for our criminals. Just because a father has committed a crime, we do not send the mother and all of the children and all of the relatives to prison!

On the other hand, these same people also say GOD is compassionate; GOD is merciful, and so on. Thus, it is very confusing to the layman as to what to believe.

I personally think it is sacrilegious to say that GOD, the Creator, is full of implacable anger and vindictiveness. But the majority of people in the world seem to believe it is acceptable to think so. They believe in hell (where we are punished eternally for our sins in this short lifetime) and heaven (where we are rewarded eternally for unquestioning obedience).

If you had such beliefs about the Creator, you would find it impossible to practice happy living, and that is the major reason why there is so much misery in the world. So it makes sense to think differently if we want to attain real happiness. So Joycentrix Rule #1 is set out as follows:

- Believe that GOD is a good and compassionate force full of unconditional love for us humans! The Creator is like a good parent who cares about the children, wants the best for them, and is happy to see them grow and fulfill their life aims and desires. Therefore, GOD is not a vindictive dictator who needs to be continually appeased with prayers, offerings, and sacrifices. GOD always has our best interests at heart.

- Believe also that GOD has created a most wonderful world for us to explore, to grow, to have fun, learn new things, make friends, go after and achieve our innermost desires, to be joyful and to spread joy, thereby fulfilling our purpose in this lifetime. At the end of this life we can then be promoted to a new dimension to continue our evolution.

- Believe also that GOD made it easy for us to live happily in this world by using our minds to understand the unchanging laws that run the universe and exploit these to solve our problems or challenges as we go after our dreams and goals.

- Believe that the universe was so set up to orchestrate all the things, people, and circumstances needed synergistically in order for you to achieve your purpose in life. Thus, GOD and the universe are for you and not against you! You do not need to appease GOD with sacrifices and offerings before you attempt any new project. GOD is well pleased when you attempt to achieve your innermost desires, which reflect your true purpose in life.

How did I come to such a conclusion that seems to be totally at odds with what religions teach? I did so simply by observation of the myriad daily phenomena in this world. Then by reasoning and deduction, it ended up becoming my acquired belief.

There are thousands of these daily phenomena we just take for granted. But if we really thought about it, we would realize these were really daily miracles! Einstein was right when he said, "We can look at everything as a miracle, or nothing as a miracle!"

I prefer to look at these daily phenomena as miracles. As I continue to be aware and begin to really think about these daily miracles, I am filled with wonder and gratitude at the unconditionally loving nature of GOD. I become convinced that GOD truly is a benevolent entity who only has our best interests at heart.

You, too, will become convinced of this if you become aware of and think deeply about everything around you that you take for granted. I invite you, dear reader, to begin conducting this experiment for yourself and uncover untold daily miracles.

It is all about taking the time to really observe some common daily occurrences that we take for granted and wonder with childlike curiosity at how miraculous these things truly are. Then you will be amazed and learn to be grateful for these daily miracles.

In order to get you started, I shall discuss a few of these daily miracles in this chapter.

Daily Miracle #1: Ice Cubes Float in Water!

The other day I was at a restaurant and observed that the ice cubes were floating on top of the fruit juice I had ordered. You say: "So what? Big deal! Ice cubes float. Anybody can see that!" However, I say that it is a big deal. It is a miracle. Think about it.

Generally any element in solid form is denser than when in the liquid form. To put it another way, all liquids expand when they are warmed up and contract when they are cooled down. This is the principle we use in our thermometers. The mercury in the thermometer tube rises as the temperature increases and vice versa.

So if we were to cool a glass of water, the colder water should sink to the bottom and the warmer water should rise to the top! So by right ice that is colder than the water (at 0 degrees Celsius) should sink to the bottom, shouldn't it?

However, water has a special property (called the anomalous property of water), whereby as it is cooled down (say from room temperature), it will initially contract until the temperature reaches 4 degrees Celsius, at which point it will start to expand. So at 0 degrees Celsius or the temperature at which ice forms, the solid ice is actually less dense than water. Thus, ice floats on water.

By the way, *anomalous* is just another word for peculiar, atypical, aberrant, abnormal, and so on, by which the scientist is simply saying, "We don't know how or why water behaves in this way. It just does!"

Even though I don't know how water does that in terms of physics or chemistry, I think I do know why GOD makes water behave in that peculiar fashion. It is because of the Creator's love for life on this planet. GOD wants to ensure that life continues to thrive! Let me explain.

Imagine what would happen to the ponds, lakes, and oceans if water behaved like other liquids and kept contracting as it gets colder. During winter the colder water at the surface of ponds would sink to the bottom, and if it continued to do so, the ice would also sink to the bottom, and the pond would tend to freeze from the bottom upward. This is true for lakes and the oceans too.

Now when summer came and started thawing the ice, only the ice close to the surface would become water, but the ice at the bottom would never get the chance to thaw out. After several winters, the pond would be frozen solid. To take it to the extreme, if this were to happen to the oceans, and they froze solid, we would be left with no marine life as well as the imminent danger of another ice age!

Because nature knows this, it made sure that water would start to expand after 4 degrees Celsius, thus causing the colder water to rise back to the surface and causing freezing from the top down. Thus, when summer comes, the ice layer on top can be melted easily by the sun and preserve marine life, which have been living safely under the ice.

This I believe is one reason why water behaves in the anomalous manner. It is because the Creator wants all living creatures (whether in the sea, on land, or in the air) to continue to have the gift of life for *as long as they need to grow and evolve* on earth. If they have completed their particular cycle of evolution, the creatures may become extinct.

*   *   *

Daily Miracle #2: This Morning Something Miraculous Happened to Me!

This morning something miraculous happened to me. *I woke up!* That's right. I said that I woke up. Isn't that miraculous? Just think about this. There I have been lying on the bed dead to the world for several hours. I have been asleep.

All my senses have shut down. My eyes are closed, and I don't see anything. My ears are open, but I don't hear anything. My sense of touch has deserted me. I don't feel the bed sheet or the blanket against my skin. I'm not even aware of my existence as an individual person. My awareness unit has gone off someplace. I don't know where.

Yet my physical body is more alive than ever. My heart continues to beat. My respiration goes on, and assimilation is ongoing. Furthermore, repair and rejuvenation are being carried out on all my cells. My brain is still filing and sorting out all the images and sense impressions I've received during the entire day. On top of all that I can also dream vividly! Isn't sleep incredible?

All of a sudden I'm awake. My senses return. I hear the myriad sounds of the newborn day—the singing of the birds, the meowing of the cat next door, the starting up of the neighbor's car. I feel the touch of cloth on skin. I open my eyes, and I see the ceiling. I realize where I am, who I am. My awareness returns!

Imagine if I had not woken up, if my awareness had not returned, if my sleep had turned into a coma or death! But I did wake up, and that is indeed a miracle.

Wow! Every morning that we wake up is indeed a miracle!

A whole new day has been given to me to do whatever I choose. Whether I choose to turn over and go to sleep again or get up, whether I start the day joyfully or mournfully, whether I desire to do great things with today or waste it—it is left entirely up to me! What a great gift, this gift of life. This morning I experienced the feeling of true gratitude. I thanked GOD and felt good. No, euphoric would be closer to the truth.

So I went downstairs and greeted my wife with a bright, "Good morning," and gave her a hug. She nearly fainted.

She asked me, "Why are you so happy today?"

I answered. "Something miraculous happened to me this morning!" and told her what I've been saying to you now.

I added, "What a thankless task it must be to be GOD!" The Creator keeps on giving without receiving any appreciation or thanks. GOD has given me more than twenty thousand days, and finally today I appreciate this gift and thank him for it.

Then she said something profound, "At least you thanked him once! Most of us never do. We just take it all for granted." How true! I wonder how many of the six billion humans on Earth ever bothered to thank GOD for their daily gift of life!

*   *   *

The final example of a daily miracle I want to record here is from a speech I gave at a Toastmasters Club meeting.

Daily Miracle #3: Thank God for My Elbows

Ladies and Gentlemen,

Hope the title caused you to pause and think! Too many of us take everything for granted. Let me relate a very moving experience I had about three years ago.

True story: I was in the town of Kuala Perlis, Kedah, in the north of Malaysia for two weeks on a technical writing job for the power station there. I was staying at the hotel just opposite the ferry terminal to the famous tourist destination Langkawi Island. One evening I was having dinner at a nearby restaurant when I noticed a group of young men at a nearby table.

Most of them were fishermen or farmers with dark weather-beaten countenances, but one young man stood out. His face was fair and finely chiseled, and he was engaged in animated conversation with the others. Then I noticed his left hand (or more correctly the lack of it)! His left arm stopped just below his elbow, ending in a stump with a few little protuberances (soft bubbles of flesh) that made up his hand.

He had no palm or fingers. Yet he was holding a cigarette in that deformed limb. When he reached down for a drink, I was stunned to observe that his right hand, too, was similar—ending in a stump with a few small appendages in place of fingers. So how did he drink? His fingers were not strong enough or long enough to hold the glass.

Fortunately his elbows were working fine. So he held the glass between both his arm stumps and by bending his elbows brought the glass to his mouth and drank as though it were the most natural thing in the world! Yet he never looked morose or dejected. In fact, he seemed to be the life of that little party.

Later when he was about to leave, I had another shock. He rolled out a motorbike (not one modified for the disabled but a regular one). When he rode away, the shopkeeper saw me looking and said to me, "Do you know that both his feet are also deformed?" I hadn't noticed because of the special shoes he wore.

Friends, can you imagine that? That was an unforgettable lesson for me on the power of living in gratitude—to be able to carry on a "normal" life in spite of such horrific disabilities! That is also when I realized the true value of my elbows! So I am not being facetious when I say, "Thank God for my elbows!" I mean it from the bottom of my heart.

Let us think about this. We see a blind man, and we think, Thank God I'm not blind. We see a cripple and say, "Thank God for my legs." But has anyone ever said, "Thank God for my elbows"? I guess not because we take for granted most things that nature has given us. We don't appreciate them enough or think about them at all. Instead of living happily each day in gratitude for all that we do have, we spend the time complaining about all that we do not have!

Imagine this scenario: If I had no elbow or if it were fused solid, how would I reach into my pocket? How would I comb my hair? This bottle of water—how would I drink? How would I brush my teeth? How would I eat? How would I use the computer? How would I write? How would I hug someone?

Isn't it incredible that without my elbows I could not do any of the thousand and one little daily actions that I take for granted? Tying a shoelace, opening an umbrella, even waving good-bye—these are all impossible without elbows! So I leave you with this thought: *Be grateful for everything that you do have, even if it seems as commonplace and unimportant as your elbows!*

Thank you.

*   *   *

The above mentioned stories are only three instances of what I mean by daily miracles. There are thousands (perhaps millions more) that demonstrate GOD's love for us.

For your own practice, here are a few more daily occurrences that you can begin to think about, wonder at, and be amazed by.

1. **Coconut Tree:** How does water from the roots reach the coconuts forty feet above ground and provide such a sweet, refreshing drink within each coconut? Even air pressure (used in a lifting pump) can only raise water up to about twenty feet or so!

2. **Dreams:** How can we touch and taste and hear and see in color as well as feel all the emotions as though it were totally real? Is a blind person able to see color in his or her dreams and a deaf person able to hear music in his or her dreams?

3. **Our Tongue:** How does it synchronize its movements while it moves food around to avoid getting chopped to pieces by the gnashing of teeth?

4. **Mind:** Where is our mind located? In the head? In the heart? Or in each cell? How?

5. **Sneeze:** Think of all the complex actions that have to take place simultaneously before we can sneeze safely.

It is by pondering on such daily occurrences that I was able to come to the conclusion that GOD is a good and compassionate force full of unconditional love for us humans. Some readers may ask, "How can I believe that GOD is a benevolent, compassionate force when we are faced with trouble and turmoil in our lives? If GOD is so benevolent, why does he allow bad things to happen?"

I have tried to answer this question at length in the next chapter under the heading "Why Does God Allow Bad Things to Happen?" which I hope will give a satisfactory answer.

CHAPTER 9

Joycentrix Rule #2: Knowing the True Nature of the World

What is the true nature of this world? According to Hindu philosophy, this world is a place for working out the karma in our previous lifetimes. According to the Bible, this place is one of punishment where we were banished to suffer because of the original sin of Adam and Eve. Some masters and teachers from the East say this world is an illusion, thus devaluing the very purpose of life.

The most general assumption and the most widespread teaching is that life is a curse and this world is one where we are forced to suffer. I beg to differ. I feel that life is a blessing and this world is a wonderful place for us to experience the fullness of life and thus evolve to a higher state.

Now let me elaborate on my belief that life is a blessing and that the universe is for us and not against us. Just try this experiment: Imagine the perfect world. What do you consider to be a perfect world? Think about it and come up with your own vision of an ideal world.

Have you done that? Now describe your own perfect world.

Next ask yourself, "Have I greater intelligence or more compassion than GOD, the omnipotent, the omniscient, and the ever-loving?"

You answer: "Of course not! How can I be more intelligent or have more compassion than GOD?"

Then obviously this world that GOD himself has created must be the perfect world—not the world that we (or many of our religious teachers), who in our own ignorance and foolish arrogance, imagine it should be!

This world is perfect for human beings at our present state of growth or evolution simply because GOD created it that way. A little story will illustrate this better.

The Wicked Man Who Loved Fishing

There was once a wicked man with no redeeming qualities whatsoever who had only one hobby—fishing. When he died, he expected to go to hell. But on his death he found himself beside a beautiful lake. He was given a lovely fishing rod. He could not believe his good fortune.

He threw the line into the water and immediately he got a fish. He was excited. He threw the line in a second time and immediately got another fish. By the end of fifteen minutes he had a basketful of fish, and he was getting really bored.

Then he realized that if he were to continue to catch a fish each time he threw in the line, it was going to be hell!

This man had enjoyed fishing only when it was challenging and exciting because he did not know if he would land a catch or not. If he was assured of a catch each time he threw in the line, then what was the point?

What is the moral of the story? The basic moral is that we as humans need challenges to overcome if we are to feel that we have achieved anything worthwhile! In life there must be challenges to make life exciting. We grow by overcoming challenges and not by avoiding them. Achievement is all the sweeter if there is struggle involved.

But the deeper moral of the story for me is that GOD is compassionate and GOD is not a vengeful dictator. The Creator knows what is good for us humans, and thus, he has created this wonderful world for us to live, experience, feel, learn, grow, enjoy, exploit our talents, and achieve our goals, thereby feeling truly fulfilled.

So the challenges we face as humans in this world are there for our growth and for our ultimate happiness, not as punishment for our transgressions by an implacable dictator!

In the last chapter I discussed why I believe GOD is a benevolent being who is for us and not against us! If GOD is for us, then logically this world he created is also for us and not against us unlike what most teachers have taught us to believe. So what can I liken this world to? Is it a penal colony where we are put as punishment for our sins and the sins of our forefathers? Is it a harsh place where we are tested by suffering and sorrow? I don't think so!

I prefer to think of the world as a learning institution—a school, college, or university rather than as a penal colony! Just think about this. Didn't we have some of our best times during our college or university days? Most of us feel nostalgic about the good old days in school, which is why we have so many annual get-togethers for old boys and past pupils.

At college we had the opportunity to learn so much, do so much, and experience so much! We could study in the libraries and classrooms. We could carry out experiments in the laboratories. We could play games and take part in athletic events, and we could learn to debate. Depending on the college, we could also swim or learn music, dancing, and acting. We could make lifelong friends, and we could even fall in love. Best of all, we could have fun doing all these!

Isn't that how the world is set up too? For us to have fun learning, doing, feeling, growing, and experiencing everything we have an interest in? What better way can there be for humans to develop and grow and exploit all their innate talents that they have been gifted with? So I believe that the world is like a wonderful institution of learning.

And what do we have to do to get promoted from year to year in a college? We have to study and carry out our assignments to the best of our abilities. Then we are sure to be promoted to the next year and so on till graduation. Do we have to constantly worry or obsess about the following questions?

- Who founded the college? How do I please him with gifts and praise?
- Why did he set up the college?
- Do I really need to study here? Real life happens after graduation. So I am only focused on how I can be sure of admission to MIT or Harvard or Oxford.

No, we don't. All we have to do is concentrate on doing a good job in the classroom and in our co-curricular activities each year, and we are sure to be promoted to the next year and ultimately get an entrance to our favorite university. Of course, if we cut classes and never carry out our assignments and only make trouble for the other students, we will not be promoted to the next year but may have to repeat the class or may even be suspended!

I feel that it is the same when it comes to living in this world. If we live a good and great and happy life in this dimension (college), we will surely be promoted to a better/higher dimension in due course. So why do we worry so much about the next life or the afterlife?

Why do we have to fantasize about what GOD is like? Just as we don't need to know who founded the college and send the founder gifts in the hope of getting good results, we don't need to appease GOD or pray for salvation. We are already on the path to salvation just by living and living well. We will elaborate on what living well means later.

Now if we don't learn our lessons in this life and refuse our worldly assignments, then it should be no surprise that we have to come back and repeat life in this dimension over and over again. Refusing to live, learn, and grow (saying that life is an illusion) is not going to make any difference. You will learn sooner or later, but you will learn! Remember that the universe has infinite time so it has infinite patience. It is not in any hurry.

If you refuse to learn all that you are supposed to learn in this lifetime, that's okay. If you refuse to follow your inner programming (or conscience), if you do not believe in the law of action and reaction (of reaping what we sow), that is okay too! Remember the universe has infinite compassion. So you are not going to be punished if you fail to learn in this lifetime.

You are not going to be sent to hell for eternity! You will be given more chances to learn—that is all. You may have to keep coming back again and again and again (if you so choose) to this world until you are ready to be promoted to the next dimension!

Our souls took on this life form in order to experience, to learn, to love, to enjoy, and hence to grow. The best way we can fulfill that purpose is to live: to think, to feel, and to experience enthusiastically with our whole heart and mind and soul.

If we remember that GOD is for us, that the world is for us, and that we humans have been programmed for happiness, it should not be difficult to make daily happy living a reality! Again you ask me, "If GOD and the universe are for us, why do bad things happen in the world?" It's a very common and very valid question indeed, one that I'll try to answer below.

Why Does GOD Allow Bad Things to Happen?—Part 1

I believe this question is one that many people keep asking because they do not understand the principle of creating and operating a system.

Consider the following true story: A few weeks ago a freak accident happened on one of the expressways of Malaysia. A bus crashed through the guardrails at the side of the road and the rails speared through the bus. This resulted in the horrific deaths of several passengers.

As usual there was a lot of mail in the newspapers saying that the guardrails should be better designed and changed and so on. Most people forgot that the true cause of the accident was the driver and not the guardrails.

As some wit once said, "The cause of any accident is always the nut behind the steering wheel."

The guardrails are not designed to keep your vehicle on the road safely if you hit it at ninety kilometers per hour or so. And they need not be! But as usual the public will blame the highway builders.

Of course, there are some cases where the highways are not designed properly, such as poor banking at road curves unable to accommodate the recommended speeds, road surface deteriorating very fast in the rainy season, high possibility of landslides, and so on. But in the vast majority of cases, the expressways in Malaysia are of a really high standard!

Why am I bringing up this incident? Because it reflects the way people think in general. They always tend to look for someone or something outside of themselves to blame. *They do not accept responsibility for their own actions.* In the case above, if the driver had been alert (not sleepy or on drugs or whatever else caused the lapse of concentration) and was driving safely, then this accident would not have occurred. To blame the road designers or the guardrails for being the main cause of the problem is ridiculous!

You should note that when a public road used by thousands is involved, there could be cases when you may end up in an accident, even if you are not to blame. Some other car can suddenly jump the divider and fall into your path. You cannot avoid the crash, and it is not your fault. But it is still the other driver's fault, not the fault of the road designer or builder!

(NOTE: Even in such a case, you might have been able to keep yourself safe if you had used your mind and your intuition correctly. For example, if you had been listening to your intuition, you may have been prompted to go slower or faster or to change lanes and thus avoided the impending accident. Personally I have been saved from being in a crash on a couple of occasions because I listened to my intuition. But most of the time, we are too busy to listen to the promptings of our intuition or sixth sense and so disregard our inner feelings, which could have helped us!)

Similarly the world, too, is designed to be of a high standard (perhaps the highest standard) by the Creator. But we have to be responsible for our own actions.

For example, in the United States especially, every day we hear of shooting-related deaths of children and other innocent people, but they are still very reluctant to pass a gun control law! It seems ridiculous to me that small kids (pre-teenagers) are involved in fatal shootings.

If they had no easy access to guns, these tragedies would not have occurred. But sadly a small percentage of adults insist on their right to bear arms and are negligent in keeping the guns out of reach of the children. So when the innocent children die, do we blame GOD or the people whose actions caused the tragedies?

Even when we talk of global events, such as climate change, is GOD really to blame? We cause the problems, and over a long period of time they escalate into a global catastrophe. Just as when we drive on the roads, we have to follow certain common sense rules to avoid accidents. So too in life we have to follow certain common sense rules to maintain the integrity of the planet.

Just as the designer of the road cannot (and should not) be held responsible for every individual driver's actions, so too GOD cannot be held responsible for the actions of each human! Each one of us has been provided with the tools (our bodies and our senses) and the ability (our brains and minds) to live a wonderful life in a truly well-designed universe. It is our responsibility to make sure we do live a wonderful life.

Another thing to remember is how universal laws work. A universal law or principle has to be true all the time and has to be neutral—not a respecter of persons! This will be discussed in part 2 below.

Why Does GOD Allow Bad Things to Happen?—Part 2

In part 1 of this topic we stated some of the reasons behind why we should not blame GOD for the bad things that happen. I ended the discussion saying that "all universal laws/principles are true all the time and are completely neutral." Now we will explore this further.

Let us take the simplest case of a well-known and documented universal law—the law of gravity. It applies to everything on earth, in our solar system, and our galaxy. On Earth nothing and no one is exempt from this universal law. The law of gravity is as true for the inanimate (air, lead, feather, rock, or water) and for the animate (humans, animals, birds, or insects). It is true for the beggar as for the millionaire, for the saint as for the sinner, for the strong as for the weak, for the philanthropist as for the terrorist.

It doesn't take sides. It remains neutral . . . always. If a terrorist and a philanthropist fell ten floors to the pavement below, both would face the same fate—smashed to death. That is obvious, so can we blame the universe for allowing the philanthropist to die?

More importantly the law of gravity must hold true **all** the time! Can you imagine what would happen if gravity were to make exceptions? Let us assume that the law of gravity was suspended for just a few seconds.

Imagine the catastrophes that could occur around the world. All things that were not firmly embedded or secured to the ground would fly off into space! The people walking on the pavement would suddenly become weightless for a few seconds and may end up a thousand feet up in the air. The atmosphere itself would be thrown off into space by the rotation of the earth. The planes flying at twenty thousand feet would suddenly be swept up to the outer layers of the atmosphere and would explode because they were not designed to fly in vacuum.

Even in the kitchen the mother pouring out boiling water from a kettle into a cup may find the stream of boiling water going upward and may get scalded. Cars on the ground would lose traction with the ground and go tumbling. There would be total chaos on earth, all because the law of gravity was suspended for a few seconds!

So now we understand why a universal law has to work all the time. We can also understand why a universal law cannot make exceptions—no matter what or who is involved. We have to learn to study, understand, and accommodate it. Thus, there is no point in blaming either the universe or the Creator for the bad things that happen!

In addition, GOD cannot or will not intervene to make exceptions once the system has been set up to run automatically! I remember thinking about this point when I was watching the 1984 Olympics on TV. During the final of the 100 meters sprint, all the eight finalists were making supplications to their own particular god before the start of the race. Some made the sign of the cross, others held their palms together, yet another bowed his head while holding his palms open, some touched the earth and brought the hand to their lips and so on.

This made me think that the runners were putting god in a quandary! Assuming god is one, how is he going to decide who should win when each of the runners are praying to him? How can he take sides and why should he? Again, if there are many gods, does it mean that the god of one religion is more powerful if the runner who prays to him was to win? Also when we think of armies at war which army is god going to favor when both pray earnestly to him?

From these thoughts I came to realize that GOD cannot and will not intercede or make exceptions for individuals. Since each one is a child of GOD, then how can he show favoritism to one over the other? The idea of god coming down to earth to answer each person's prayers just because he is pleased with the rituals prescribed by religions is too far-fetched. This idea which is so popular (in fact it is the norm amongst the majority of people) is more suited to fables like Cinderella or Aladdin where a fairy godmother or a genie turns up to make everything right. This subject of 'why most prayers are not answered and why only some are answered' is too vast for me to expand on in this book.

Suffice it to say that GOD has given each human being the power to create his own reality in terms of material surroundings and circumstances by utilizing the incredible power of his mind as well as the universal mind (described in the next chapter)! A person can achieve his dreams and goals by his faith and by putting his focus on his goal and by taking relevant action, whenever his intuition prompts him to do so! He does not need to pray for god's intercession. All that he needs is already provided for him; he only needs to reach out and welcome it and not push it away by doubt and negative beliefs. (The only form of prayer needed is that of thanksgiving where when we thank GOD or the Universe for the gifts we are given daily.)

Another practical reason why a universal law must work all the time is to enable human beings to study the law and work with it. If the force of gravity were to change at random, the scientists would not be able to utilize this force for other purposes, including the following:

- *Flying an aircraft.* We need to be able to balance the downward force of gravity with the upward force of the air and the forward thrust of the jet engine. It is because we know that the force of gravity is constant and calculable that we are able to utilize this law to fly.

- *Sending up a satellite into space.* This, too, is possible only because we can calculate how much thrust we need to propel the rocket at such a speed to overcome the force of gravity and thus exceed the escape velocity of earth so as to launch into space.

In any earthly system for the many, individuals have to follow certain rules to make it work. If the individuals are not following the rules, it is they who are ultimately responsible for the bad things that happen, not the one who created the system!

Of course, when it comes to systems created by us humans, there will be shortcomings, but when we talk of a system created by GOD, even something as complex as this planet and its people, it is bound to be perfect. There is no chance of shortcomings. For example, consider the following:

- The beauty and harmony between plants and animals: The respiration of the animals (which gives out CO_2) is balanced out by the photosynthesis of plants (which gives out O_2).

- The water cycle of nature: Surface water evaporates (distilling the water), is collected as clouds, and comes down as rain to become surface water again.

- The anomalous behavior of water: This allows solid ice to be lighter than liquid water, thus allowing ice to float and thereby preserving ocean life and life on earth. (Note that this has been described in chapter 8 under Daily Miracle #1.)

The only shortcomings are caused by us in our ignorance of the universal laws and oftentimes by our deliberate attempts to circumvent some of these laws because of our greed and selfishness (e.g., over logging, destroying trees and vegetation for buildings, changing the balance of CO_2 and O_2 in the atmosphere by burning fossils, destroying the protective ozone layer).

In conclusion, the question "Why does GOD allow bad things to happen?" only shows that we lack understanding of the world and the unchangeable universal laws that have been put in place for the protection of the planet and its people by the Creator.

GOD does not intervene or intercede in any way to make either bad things or good things happen!

If GOD intervened at every step, then what would be the need for giving free will to humans? GOD has created a perfect system that is designed to run and maintain and heal itself if left on its own. However, we have been given the power to co-create, and this is bound to have an impact on the preservation of the planet. Whether this impact is positive or negative depends on us humans and how we use this power.

GOD has prepared a wonderful place for us humans to experience, learn, have fun, grow, and use our free will, our minds, and all the creative powers we have been gifted with. Whether our co-creation turns out good or bad depends almost entirely on us. As humans we should be taking charge and accepting responsibility for our own actions and we should stop blaming GOD, other people, or outward circumstances!

In summary, let me reiterate my beliefs about the world as stated in Joycentrix Rule #2:

- *This world is a supportive place that enables humans to evolve, not a place of punishment or a penitentiary.* I believe that this world is like a school or university! It is *not* a prison where we are forced to suffer as punishment for our past sins. Instead the world is a wonderful place of education and development with all the facilities (such as libraries, labs, playing fields, swimming pools, etc.) for us to learn, grow, make friends, and have fun.

- *I believe that living in this world is like being in a particular class or form!* If I do well in say form one, then I will be promoted to form two automatically. If, on the other hand, I do badly in this class, I may have to come back to repeat the class! And remember that the universe has infinite time. It can allow me to repeat the same class a hundred or a thousand times. (This we call reincarnation or living several lifetimes.)

- *So I believe that my only priority in life is to live well.* If I lead a great, fulfilled life here, I do not have to worry about the afterlife or fear it! I will be promoted to the next dimension in good time, and that place, too, will be good!

CHAPTER 10

Joycentrix Rule #3: Knowing the Nature of the Mind

Philosophers, psychologists, and scientists have been interested in the nature of the mind for centuries. However, it is only in the last two hundred years or so that we have begun to gain some understanding of the immense power and complexity of our minds. We learned that our minds have at least two parts—the conscious and the subconscious. The conscious part has only a fraction of the power and ability of the subconscious and so on. Since so much has already been said and written about these two aspects of the mind, we will not elaborate further upon this.

Instead I would like to discuss a third part of the mind—the universal mind! This is what Emerson called "the oversoul" more than 150 years ago. He believed that each individual soul is a part of the oversoul—the unity of all souls. While I think Emerson's essays on the oversoul and self-reliance two of the best essays I have ever read, his views seem somewhat mystical.

Therefore, I would like to look at the oversoul concept in a more practical way. Since I am fortunate to be born in this time and age when the radio, Internet, and cellular phones are so common, this gives me a simple analogy to explain the oversoul or universal mind concept.

It is easy and natural for me to think of my mind as a powerful receiver of thoughts and feelings as compared with the radio receiver. Just as it is possible for me to receive wireless signals from the ether by tuning the radio to a particular frequency, it is also possible for me to receive thoughts and feelings from the universal mind. Furthermore, our minds also have the power to transmit thoughts and feelings. (Think of the cell phone, which we can use to transmit our voice to anywhere in the world.)

The universal mind can be likened to the Internet or World Wide Web. Just as it is possible for me to log on to the Internet, it is also possible for me to transmit my thoughts and feelings to the universal mind. All this and more (such as distance healing), is possible for each mind, but we are not yet fully aware of how to do it consciously and by design.

Fortunately we don't have to delve into the theory of the mind before we put our mind to practical use. We can use our mind in very simple and practical ways to achieve our intentions. I have included several happy living tips in this book, and this seems to be the ideal juncture at which to introduce one of these, namely "Creating a Happiness Aura."

This describes a practical means of changing our aura, thereby changing how we affect others, which leads to better communications.

Happy Living Tip#1: Creating a Happiness Aura

Whether we can see it or not and whether we believe it or not, each one of us has an aura that we carry about with us all the time! And this aura affects everyone who we come into contact with. This is easy to prove.

Hasn't each one of us at one time or another just met someone and immediately warmed up to him or her even before we started up a conversation? The opposite is also true. We have also met those whom we felt like avoiding even before we have spoken to them.

Why is that? Simply because each one of us carries an aura that is like a force field around us, one that is not seen but can be felt by others.

When we are morose and depressed, we carry about a negative aura that repels people, and when we are happy, our aura attracts others. This has been well studied and documented, so we are not talking something new here. You can even have your own aural photograph taken at many alternative therapy establishments.

So the question now is this: "How do I create a happiness aura?"

Since our aura is based on our feelings, the way to change our aura is to change our feelings, and the way to change our feelings is to change our thoughts. And one simple way of changing our thoughts and thereby our feelings is through affirmations repeated with strong feeling.

A favorite affirmation I use before I attend any gathering, meeting, or seminar is this: "I spread goodness, goodwill, cheer, and prosperity wherever I go and wherever I am!"

When I repeat this affirmation to myself a couple of times and think intently about each word (goodness, goodwill, cheer) and feel the emotion attached to each word, I feel much happier. I also change my intention from just attending a meeting to really spreading happiness and cheer when I am there. This creates a happiness aura around me!

The results are incredible, especially for me because I am not the outgoing type at all. Not only that, my demeanor is too solemn and unsmiling—so much so that even strangers remark, "Why do you look so serious?" In fact, my dear wife once remarked, "Your facial expression is more suitable for funerals, not weddings!"

But even so I have found time and again that whenever I go to any gathering with a happiness aura, I get two delightful results:

1. I am able to greet people very cordially and build rapport easily, and
2. I find that people seem more approachable and friendly. They also seem to really like me.

On the other side of the coin, when I forget to create my happiness aura (by using this affirmation), I go back to my normal, saturnine self and find it difficult to communicate easily with others. The others then return the favor by being less cooperative or even difficult.

So that is Happiness Tip #1, whereby you can create a happiness aura whenever you need to meet others, thus setting up easier and more cordial pathways to communication. If we can do this habitually all the time, then our aura would become so attractive that we would be welcome anywhere at any time.

*   *   *

I began this topic about the nature of the mind with the human aura because it is very easily demonstrated. However, the human aura extends only a few feet in radius around our body, whereas the mind is capable of connecting with people all over the world.

This should not seem surprising to us at the present time when even human inventions like the cellular phone have global reach. Imagine how much more powerful and far-reaching would be the mind, which is GOD's creation!

In fact, there is no space-time restriction on the human mind in its ability to connect with either the universal mind or other individual minds. This explains extrasensory perception (ESP), premonitions, intuition, and so on. Some of these phenomena that seem magical are all part and parcel of nature. We humans are only just beginning to understand some of these powers and learning to control them.

We are still a long way off when compared to the majesty of GOD's creations, but we are getting more and more adept at imitating GOD. (The computer, the wireless, the cell phone, and the Internet are just modest imitations of our brains, minds, and the universal mind respectively.)

This analogy of the Internet to universal mind is very useful in explaining many of the seemingly miraculous powers of the mind. For example, let us take the case of us setting a goal, overcoming challenges, and finally achieving it.

Goal Setting and Goal Achieving

If I decide to start a business online (say one that focuses on weight loss), there are certain steps that I need to follow in order to make it work. First I search the term *weight loss* on the search engines and come up with thousands of topics related to weight loss. Then I have to sift through the many results and choose which particular niche I am going to focus on. Once I have decided on my niche, then I create a general plan and learn about getting weight-loss products to sell, creating websites, promoting online, and so on. I try many approaches until I finally make a success of that business online.

In the real world too there are similarities. Once I focus constantly on a dream goal or purpose with belief and confidence, then I am beginning to transmit thought messages to the universal mind, and the search begins! Initially I may get many different ideas that may seem irrelevant (similar to the search results on Google). Then when I continue to focus, I will start getting very relevant ideas that I can easily implement.

The universal mind is connected to all things and is therefore able to orchestrate everything (the people, ideas, and circumstances) that I need in order to make my dream goal a reality. It does this by giving me flashes of intuition or inspiration. My only job is to stay focused and take action on my intuitions.

In the beginning my intuitions may not be spot on since I am just learning to use these extra powers of my mind, and several of my intuitions may not be genuine and only the result of my wishful thinking. But if I remain steadfast to my goal and make the necessary corrections whenever I go wrong, I will find it easier and easier to read my genuine intuitive messages and act upon them.

Soon I will find synergistic happenings and lucky breaks that help me achieve my goal easier. Things such as unexpected calls, surprise meetings, a random e-mail that reveals just what I need, and other things will soon become a regular affair. Friends and relatives will be amazed at how much I am able to accomplish in a short time.

The above scenario is true for each and every one of us no matter what our dream or goal is. Our goal could be becoming a world-class athlete, a pianist, a healer, or an entrepreneur. It does not matter as long as we focus on our goal and begin to take action on our inspirations—even if the actions initially result in failure. This also applies if our goal is happiness, which is what this book is all about.

How Is the Universal Mind Able to Create Synchronicity for Us?

I believe that the oversoul or universal mind is the seat of all knowledge—past, present, and future. Hence, it is able to see things that our individual minds are unable to see. It is all a matter of perspective as I shall describe below.

Imagine you are driving in a strange town. You are lost on an unknown street. The buildings towering above you on all sides block your view, and you can't get your bearings. You have very limited perspective. Now imagine you had a friend on a high-rise building and he is able to see your car and talk to you on your cell phone. His perspective is much wider, and he can direct you better; however, even his perspective is somewhat limited because once your car turns the corner he can't see you. However, if you are getting directions through a GPS from a satellite several miles up in the sky (with a global perspective), then you will not get lost.

Another good example of differing perspectives that enable one to even predict a future outcome is using a weather satellite. From the satellite photos we are able to see a hurricane forming in the middle of the ocean; we are able to calculate its speed and can predict precisely just when it will make landfall in a particular state or city. Thus, it is not really a prediction but a calculated forecast.

However, if we did not know about weather satellites, then it would seem like a miracle to us when someone predicts that a hurricane is bound to hit our city in exactly four hours, especially if we are experiencing calm and clear skies now.

We have all read about how certain explorers in the past managed to impress primitive tribes into thinking they were gods just because they could forecast an eclipse of the sun! To the primitive tribes, the onset of sudden darkness in the daytime was a miracle brought on by the gods, but we know that it was an anticipated phenomenon whose time was already calculated in the almanac.

Similarly the oversoul has universal perspective. Hence, it is able to show you the best possible route to take for you to reach your goal in the fastest and easiest way. It is also able to arrange conditions that are favorable to you. All you need to do is learn how to listen to its instructions. Some people do it by meditation, others by being aware of their intuitive flashes and acting confidently on these.

The question once again is this: "Do you believe that the world is for you or against you?" If you believe it is for you, then you will find it easy to reach your goals. If you believe the world is against you, then the power of your belief will create a reality that is difficult. As I said before, the universal laws are neutral, and belief is a universal law. So choose your beliefs wisely and well.

Since this book is dedicated to make happy living a practical reality, I don't wish to engage in further theoretical discussion on the nature of the mind, which is a huge subject and one I am not really qualified to speak on. Thus, the short and simple comparison above (of the oversoul to the Internet and the mind to a transmitter and receiver) should be sufficient to give the reader an idea of just how powerful and how complex our minds are.

Summary

In this chapter we elaborated on Joycentrix Rule #3, which is all about how we can use our minds to create our own happiness. The relevant beliefs are listed below:

- *I believe that our minds have the power to create our reality!* As stated earlier, our beliefs create our reality. And our minds can be used to formulate our beliefs. Hence, our minds can create our individual reality. Rather than just accepting any mediocre life, we have the power to design our own happy, successful lives!

- *I believe that the mind is much more than the brain!* Awareness is much more than the five senses or the intellect. The mind includes feelings and emotion. Feelings are unseen, and emotions are not measurable; however, no one can deny they do exist.

- *I believe that the powers of the mind are tremendous!* In fact, we have barely scratched the surface with all our studies in psychiatry and psychology and medicine. We are only just beginning to understand the true awesome power of our minds!

- *I believe that there are certain unalterable laws of the mind!* For example, there is one particular law of mind that works for everyone. "What we focus our thoughts on and believe in wholeheartedly is what we create in our reality!"

It works for bad as well as good. If we focus constantly on sickness (talk about it, read about it, think about it), we will get sick! If we constantly focus on health, refusing to dwell on opposing thoughts, then we can realize health!

If we focus with confidence on achieving our goals without allowing any doubtful thoughts, then we will achieve our goals! Similarly if we focus our awareness and our thoughts on happiness and joy, then this is what we will achieve.

CHAPTER 11

Joycentrix Rule #4: Knowing the Truth about Creation, Evolution, and Co-creation

About GOD

Before I talk of creation, evolution, and co-creation, I need to clarify what I believe to be GOD. I believe in a GOD who existed long before humans existed, long before humans could even communicate with each other, long before languages were created, and long before humans organized religions. Thus, I believe in a GOD who made man and not in a God or gods made by man. To separate the original Creator or the Source from the man-made gods of mythology and theology, I use the term GOD as opposed to God.

Most people like to think of God as a person who lives at some locations (this cave or that mountain) on this planet or elsewhere. My wife, too, belongs to that vast group of people who say they need to imagine God as a person or object who lives at various holy places on this planet.

> NOTE: Our differing beliefs are not a bone of contention between me and my wife since we accept each other as individuals with our own ways of thinking. Just for the record, we have been married for close to forty years! This proves that we do not have to fight others just because they have differing views of life. We can live together in harmony no matter how differing our beliefs—provided that we are willing to really accept the others as they are.

However, it seems to me very limiting to think of GOD as a person, considering the infinite vastness of the universe where our planet is only one of many in our own solar system. When I consider that each star is a sun that can have several planets in its own solar system and that there are millions of stars in this very galaxy and that there are countless galaxies in the universe, then I begin to have an idea of what infinity means! Now to imagine the Creator of all this vastness is living on top of a mountain on this planet Earth seems truly far-fetched to me.

I prefer to think of the Creator as intelligent energy that permeates through all space and matter. Perhaps because I have spent my entire professional life in the electrical industry, it is not difficult for me to imagine the Creator as a force or energy.

Even though we can't see electricity or magnetism, we accept that these forms of energy do exist by observing the results. However, neither of these forms of energy contains any selective intelligence! They just act, and in order to provide appropriate results, they need to be controlled by external forces. In contrast, it is easy for me to imagine GOD as energy that has its own intelligence.

Just as electricity is the one energy (that you cannot see) but flows through all the different appliances in your home and creates differing forms (light in the lamp, cold in the refrigerator, warmth in the heater, rotation in the washing machine, and so on), so too is GOD energy flowing through everything. Only the forms are different, but the underlying principle is the same!

It is GOD energy that allows a seed to grow into a tree or a fertilized cell to grow into a baby. It is GOD energy that keeps us alive. The moment we die, the GOD energy leaves, and the body immediately begins to decay!

So when we think of GOD as intelligent energy, it becomes easier to understand why GOD is in everything animate and inanimate as well as in the psychic realm. Our thoughts come from this one Source, and so do our feelings. In fact, this is what the philosophers mean when they talk about the unity of life.

But this does not mean that we are all the same as many teachers falsely infer! Just because the electricity that flows through all the appliances is the same, it does not mean that the washing machine is the same as a light bulb or a refrigerator the same as an oven.

Similarly each one of us humans is a separate individual who is activated by the same GOD energy—that is all. When we are in this dimension of time and space, we are unique individuals who have been gifted with the power of choice and the power of mind to make those choices become realities. Other teachers claim that each of us is GOD, but this, too, cannot logically be true.

Truthfully there is some of the GOD energy within us, but we are not GOD just as an electric appliance uses electric energy but is not electricity!

Under normal circumstances it is simply not possible for anyone to accept that you and your spouse or your mother or your friends are the same person as many great teachers ask us to believe. Each one of us is a different and unique aspect of GOD, but we are not GOD. Our only purpose in this life is to live in joy and spread the joy while we fulfill our innermost dreams by using the powers of our minds, which GOD has gifted us with.

If we think of GOD as intelligent energy, then we should not attribute male or female attributes to GOD. Just as we would not call electricity or gravity he or she but rather it, so too it makes sense for us to use the pronoun *it* to represent GOD. (However, I too am guilty of following convention and have used the pronouns 'him' and 'he' at times earlier in this book.)

> NOTE: An advantage of using *it* instead of *he* as a pronoun for GOD is that I am able to steer clear of the male chauvinistic traditions of almost all religions! All religions seem to perpetuate the arrogant notion that God must be male, thereby relegating woman to an inferior position! Thus, if we use *it* instead of *he* for GOD, we don't have to condone the subservience of women or treat women as the second sex but as equals.

About Creation

The first truth about creation is that it is ongoing. It has not ended. GOD has not gone to sleep or retired after seven days. The following is what I believe is true about creation:

1. **Macro Creation:** GOD does all the creation of matter that we can see—the planets, the suns, the stars, the solar systems, and

the galaxies. At our present level of evolution we humans have no part in this creation of the macro systems.

2. **Micro Creation:** GOD also does all the creation of the smallest particles of matter and energy that we cannot see. At our present level of evolution we also have no part in this micro creation.

3. **Psychic Creation:** GOD has also created the superlative world of the unseen, which gives rise to the mind, the world of feelings, imagination, belief, and intellect. Psychic creation and the powers of the mind are under GOD's control. At our present level of evolution *we have a small part* in this psychic creation. We cannot change these powers of the mind. We can only use these tremendous powers for human creation as outlined in the next point.

4. **Human Creation or Co-creation:** This is what we can do, and this is what we should do! GOD has given us this power so that we can become a co-creator with it and help in the evolution of mankind. We can create on a human level by combining matter that already exists into different forms by using our mind power. Our direction is provided by our feelings.

While GOD carries on the macro and micro creation, we humans have been tasked with co-creation (the managing of this university called Earth), and we have been given the powers necessary to co-create and help evolution on this planet.

This is the perfect world for us (in our present stage of evolution) to live, create, and enjoy experiences. GOD has made it as perfect as any system can be to self-regenerate, to grow, to expand, and to evolve.

GOD has given us water in the form of rain, rivers, oceans, clouds, ice, and glaciers. GOD has given us a controlled climate and the seasons. It has given us the plant kingdom and the animal kingdom to work in harmony with each other. The waste of the animal kingdom (such as CO_2) is food for the plants; waste for the plants (O_2) is vital food for the animals!

In such a way has GOD created the world that it created ecology long before we coined a word for it! It has given us minds—ones so powerful and unique that even our most advanced computers of this time can never do what one mind can do. It has so designed the world that we can create our own reality! GOD has given us some of GOD's own powers and made us co-creators!

Yet we say this world is illusion and we should avoid living in it. What convoluted thinking and what a perverse way of thanking GOD—to call its creation an illusion and therefore of no purpose. Can we really think of or imagine a better world than the one GOD has created?

Let me reiterate: this world is perfect for humans at our present stage of evolution. When we are ready for the next level, then we will be promoted to that world, which will also be perfect for us at that stage of our evolution!

GOD created desire as motivation, as a starting point for all achievement so that we can go after what we desire and in the process expand ourselves, learn new experiences, and thus grow fully.

But some of our teachers say, "Desire is the starting point of all sorrow!" They do not expect us to be able to achieve anything we desire, so they think all desires will lead to disappointment or sorrow. Yet if we observe carefully, we can see the wonderful results achieved by people who have followed their innermost desires.

The reason why these teachers preach such errors is because they have not understood how the world is run and how it works. They are unaware of what is described here about macro creation, micro creation, co-creation, or the amazing power of our mind.

However, we do have limitations. We cannot do anything to get the sun to rise up in the west (i.e., cause the earth to rotate in the opposite way or create a new star or even an ounce of matter or new DNA by ourselves).

We can only manipulate existing matter to create different forms by using the powers of our mind. But even this co-creation can be truly fabulous if we but use our full power—as we can see by the enduring architecture, great music, great literature, great inventions, etc., that we humans have achieved.

We know this to be true because we revere and are inspired by those great architects, music composers, engineers, inventors, actors, writers, and so on. We acknowledge their achievements because we know they are doing what they are destined to do with their lives.

Of course, the other side of the coin is that we can use our great powers to destroy, to maim, to enslave, and so on, and many of us have also chosen to do so. But we have done so because of fear, because of ignorance, because we do not believe that GOD is always for us.

The truth is that GOD is always for us and always have been! It is not against us. It is not standing in judgment of us. It created this world and all its beauty for us to enjoy in peace and harmony. GOD has not forbidden us from luxuries or from doing what we truly love to do.

Yet because we have been taught that GOD has forbidden us from all the good things in life, we feel that the only way to get enjoyment from life is to sell our soul to the Devil. Even if the Devil is real, why would we want to sell our souls to him and not to GOD? After all, according to the Bible, since GOD is supposed to have created the Devil, then obviously the Devil is the lesser entity.

About Evolution and Co-creation

Personally I believe that evolution is part and parcel of creation! Believing in evolution does not mean that we have to stop believing in GOD as many people seem to think. The way I see it, there is no contradiction here. Evolution is a necessary part of creation, not separate from it.

As described in an earlier paragraph, human co-creation is what helps in the evolution of the world. By creating newer and more comfortable habitats, better communication, better transport, we are helping the world evolve. If not, we would be still living in caves and hunting animals for subsistence. There is nothing wrong in evolving to higher levels. (In fact, it is nature's intention for us to grow.) Only we need to do it in a balanced manner.

This very thought was stated (more than a hundred years ago) beautifully by Wallace D. Wattles in his masterpiece *The Science of Getting Rich* in the very first chapter:

> "Every person naturally wants to become all that he/she is capable of becoming. This desire to realize innate possibilities is inherent in human nature; we cannot help wanting to be all that we can be. There are three motives for which we live: we live for the body, we live for the mind, and we live for the soul.

"No one of these is better or holier than the other; all are alike desirable, and no one of the three—body, mind, or soul—can live fully if either of the others is cut short of full life and expression. It is not right or noble to live only for the soul and deny mind or body, and it is wrong to live purely for the intellect and deny body or soul." (Wallace Wattles)

Now that we have covered the four cardinal rules of the Joycentrix System, we shall go on to discuss the all-important Cardinal Rule #5, "Knowing the Truth about Happiness," in the very next chapter.

CHAPTER 12

Joycentrix Rule #5: Knowing the Truth about Happiness

In this chapter I am going to discuss several truths about happiness. These are listed below and will be explored in detail in subsequent sections of this chapter.

1. Happiness is a choice we can make daily that becomes a habit.
2. Happiness is created within us.
3. We are programmed for joy.
4. Happiness can be enhanced (by changing our circumstances) once we already know how to be happy in spite of circumstances.

Truth #1: Happiness Is a Choice We Make Daily so that It Becomes Habit.

Abe Lincoln said, "Happiness is a habit," but I have to add "Happiness is first of all a choice, which by regular usage becomes a habit."

What do I mean by happiness being a choice? Do we really have a choice? Let us explore this question further.

Most of us go around asking: "How can I be happy when he makes me angry? How can I be happy when my job makes me frustrated? How can I be happy when my spouse does not support me?"

We always assume that it is the other party that makes us angry or upset as though we have no choice in the matter. But is that really true? Do you get angry just because of the other's actions, or is it really something else?

Let us take a simple daily example that makes us upset, even furious at times. I am talking about discourtesy on the road that causes some of us to experience undue anger to the point of road rage! To make it even more compelling, let me relate my own personal story of how I overcame my own road rage.

How I Overcame My Road Rage Almost Overnight

For years I used to feel excessive anger when other drivers were discourteous on the road. Let me tell you why. Have you heard of the Golden Rule? The Golden Rule says, "Do unto others as you would have them do unto you!" Or the reverse "Don't do unto others what you wouldn't want them to do to you!"

I used to follow the Golden Rule religiously. (In fact, I still do.) Unfortunately this meant that I expected others to do likewise! And when they did not do so, it made me furious. Perhaps you can call this affliction the Golden Rule syndrome.

Anyway, whenever I drove, I made it a point to be courteous on the road. I never double-parked, even though it meant me having to walk some distance. I always used the signals when I was changing lanes. I never hogged the fast lane. I kept an eye on the rearview mirror, and if I saw any car coming up fast behind me, I immediately gave way.

So when I saw others breaking all these basic rules of road courtesy, I used to get really mad. I am not happy about it, but to show you the extent of my affliction, I have the following confession to make.

> One thing I never do is park in front of another's driveway or gate even if it belongs to a friend I am visiting. I just could never understand why people would do that, especially when parking space was available nearby. I had even instructed my wife to tell her friends never to obstruct our gate, but she never took it seriously. She was more worried about what they would think if she told them that.

> One day I came back from work and saw a small car blocking half of the entrance to my driveway. I was upset because there was ample space in front for the car to be parked without obstructing the gate. So instead of tooting the horn and waiting for the car to be moved, I impatiently tried to squeeze my car into the driveway, and bang! The rear of my car hit the gate post and suffered a bad dent.

> My wife and the friend came rushing out of the house, looking shocked. The dent cost me several hundred dollars, which I could ill afford, but I still chose to blame the problem on my wife and her friend and not on my decision to try to squeeze my car in!

So now you know that I did have a bad case of the Golden Rule syndrome, and it would not be easy to cure me. However, I did manage to cure myself (almost overnight) of my excessive road anger, and nowadays I have no problem on the road in the face of traffic jams or driver discourtesy.

Would you like to know how I accomplished this? It came about because of two specific incidents. The first was an epiphany I had, and the second was a strange but practical tip I received from an online forum. I later spoke about this insight at a Toastmasters meeting under the title "You Control Your Thoughts, No One Else!"

You Control Your Thoughts, No One Else!

Ladies and gentlemen, tonight I am going to prove to you that it is you alone who controls your thoughts, no one else!

Let us say you get mild road rage when a car cuts in front of you suddenly and you have to apply emergency brakes to avoid ramming into it. You become furious and feel justified in expressing your rage as I used to! You rant and rave and chase after the car, overtake it, and then cut in front of that car to teach him a lesson.

So what have you gained? Have you taught the other driver never to cut in front of others suddenly? Or have you just enraged him further? You justify your actions, saying you have the right to be angry and there is nothing else you can do logically. After all, it is his fault for nearly causing an accident, and he should be taught a lesson, and so on.

But I tell you that it is not the other driver who made you mad. It is you who chose to get angry because you believed that it was the right thing to do! You gave yourself permission to cultivate thoughts of anger in your mind.

I shall prove it to you conclusively that you were still in control of your thoughts. You could have chosen to think differently and react otherwise. As an example, let us imagine this scenario: After hearing you complain endlessly about how difficult it is on the road with bad drivers, a tycoon (say Bill Gates) offers you a one-million-dollar challenge on certain conditions. The agreement is that he will give you the money in six months' time, provided that in those six months at least ten drivers had cut into your path suddenly, causing you to apply your emergency brakes, without any provocation on your part. Your car would be set up with cameras and audio (like in the police programs on TV) so that there is proof.

With this motivation I can guarantee that you will be looking forward to road hogs, especially if you have already met eight of them and there is only one week left for the six-month period to expire! You will be praying for the final two more road hogs who will make you a millionaire! In fact, you may end up cursing the good drivers!

So what changed? Your perception and your motivation! You end up praying for something that you normally would have hated and would have driven you into a rage. This proves that you need not get angry and fly into a rage when you meet a road hog. *You choose to get mad because you think that is the appropriate reaction!*

Now think about this: How much energy do we waste every day in such unfruitful matters? Is it any wonder that we are not as successful as we would like to be? If all the energy we waste on anger and vindictiveness could have been diverted into more productive channels, perhaps we could have made that million dollars by our own efforts in the next six or twelve months!

So I believe that with this example I have proven that it is possible for us to respond rationally rather than react instinctively and inappropriately.

It is really you who control your thoughts (and thus your actions), no one else!

Ladies and gentlemen, thank you.

*   *   *

That was the first realization that got me thinking perhaps I could overcome my own excessive anger on the roads. And it did help me to know that it was I who was choosing to get angry. I was not being forced by the other to respond with anger.

But it was the addition of a second idea, which I call the "bless-you technique," that helped me overcome road rage almost instantly. Actually I read about it in a forum titled *The Science of Getting Rich*, and here is an excerpt of my post in that forum about my experience:

> I would like to end with a little experience I have had since being involved in this forum. Formerly I used to have road rage. When a car cuts me off without signaling and causes me to apply the brakes suddenly, I would get so angry I would chase the offending car and cut in front of him, causing him to apply emergency brakes—tit for tat!

> Otherwise I would spend hours fantasizing how to get back at the offender and "teach him a lesson" without getting into trouble with the police!

A few months ago I happened to read a post where someone said that "they bless every person or thing that annoys or upsets them" just to maintain their own peace of mind.

So the next time when a discourteous driver cut into my lane, I happened to say just as a joke, "Bless you!"

Saying that made me laugh, thinking, here *someone has cut suddenly into my path, and I'm blessing him!* But the result was unexpected. By laughing I found that my anger had abated. I told my family about this technique, and they reminded me to use it whenever I was driving, which I tried to do as often as I could.

One day I asked myself, *if I can bless those who are driving badly, then how much more should I bless those who drive well?* So now I just bless everyone on the road (whenever I remember to).

Today I have no trouble at all on the road. Of course, being human, I do get upset occasionally (out of habit), but I am now able to get back into a tranquil state within seconds instead of wallowing in anger for an hour. Traffic jams used to bother me to no end. Now I just take it in my stride and get home in a great mood.

May I suggest that you too give the 'bless-you' technique a try when next something or someone upsets you. You may be pleasantly surprised at the resulting change of mood you experience!

This is because it feels nicer to bless rather than curse someone, even if you say it within yourself and not to his or her face. The other person does not have to hear your words. The word bless has positive connotations and is happiness-inducing, whereas the word curse automatically brings up anger, hate, and other negative feelings. Thus, the latter is not conducive to happiness.

So whenever you are faced with a circumstance that prompts you to say, "Curse you," instead choose to say, "Bless you." Remember that when you say, "Bless you," it is not for the other's benefit but selfishly for your own. When you say, "Bless you," it is you who feel good, you who feel happy, and you who benefit the most.

That brings us back to the topic of this chapter, which is that happiness is a choice that each one of us can make on a daily basis. We realize from the above mentioned stories that we are in total control of the thoughts we allow to inhabit our mind. We can choose our thoughts no matter what the outward circumstance. Hence, we can just as easily choose to think happy thoughts instead of misery-making thoughts of anger, revenge, and the like.

When I realized that I could choose not to be angry, it was a great turning point in my life. I understood then that I was only creating more stress for myself with my anger, which could affect my immune system and make me more susceptible to illness.

As a matter of fact, I used to suffer from monthly episodes of the common cold or the flu in spite of regular medication and nutritional supplements. Thankfully I don't catch cold so easily now. In fact, I am much healthier in my sixties than I was in my forties and fifties! I believe that it has a lot to do with my habitually choosing to think happy thoughts rather than giving way to anger or thinking of misery.

That simple insight about having the ability to choose our thoughts gave me the power to respond instead of just reacting to an external stimulus. But it was not easy to change a lifelong habit. I had to be persistent in choosing new thoughts each time I was faced with a discourteous driver.

My instinct would be to get angry, but I kept asking myself, "Gopi, who is in control of your mind?" On getting the answer, "I am and no one else," I was able to stop my thoughts from going wild and to quickly come back to a peaceful state.

After a while of practicing this, it became a habit. Nowadays when I think back to those days when I was filled with rage at little things, I am shocked at how I managed to live in that state for so long!

When I think of the unnecessary stress I caused my body and mind by seething with anger and vengeful thoughts for hours at a time, I am grateful for this wonderful insight that we are free to choose our thoughts no matter what the circumstances. If we are free to choose our thoughts, then there is nothing to stop us from choosing to think happy thoughts!

So happiness is a choice we make on a daily basis, which then becomes habit.

In summary, remember the following points of this chapter:

- *Believe that happiness is a choice.* So is sorrow. So is anger. So is love. What we decide to focus on in our minds is what we end up feeling and experiencing.

- *Believe that if we choose love, we will be happiest.* I am talking of unconditional love here and not reciprocal love. The second type of love (as extolled in the romances of Mills & Boon) can give happiness but can also give rise to misery if it is not reciprocated. However, unconditional love (like that which we feel when we look at an infant, a pet, and so on) is not based on reciprocation. We do not expect the infant to smile for us or dance for us to be worthy of our love; we just love with no expectation of reward.

- *Believe that pleasure (short-term happiness) is of the senses while joy and peace of mind (long-term happiness) is based on the thoughts we cultivate in our mind!* We know full well that our senses can give us pleasure immediately without any thinking being involved. Hearing a haunting melody, biting into a juicy, ripe red apple, seeing a beautiful sunset, the aroma of a special perfume; the hug of a loved one—all these can instantly make us feel happy!

But it is our attitude of mind that gives long-term happiness or peace of mind. For example, imagine you have just received news of the death of a close family member. Would you then be able to find pleasure in eating the fruit? Or in seeing the sunset? Or in hearing the melody? No! Because pleasure is of the senses, but real happiness (joy) is of the mind!

Truth #2: Happiness Can Be Created within Each One of Us on a Daily Basis.

How can we create happiness within us? Merely by being aware of our feelings and being aware of the thoughts that brought about those feelings and then choosing the thoughts that will leave us feeling good and truly happy.

Thus, the first step to creating happiness is to be aware when you are not. In fact, I would even go so far as to say, "The secret to being happy is to be aware when you are not!"

Coming back to the statement above, I can hear you saying, "Of course I am aware when I am not happy! What on earth are you talking about?"

Remember that I'm not talking about real, in-your-face sort of tragic events, such as bereavement, separation, being laid off, and so on. In these cases you know you are unhappy—no two ways about it! However, most of the time, we rankle with unhappiness inside and don't even know it.

Well, just think about it. Are you really aware when you are unhappy at the instant that you feel upset? Normally we are not. What we do is we allow all the little irritations to build up in our minds, and over time we feel bad and don't know why. We blame it on our moods.

But a mood is not just something that appears out of the blue. It is the sum of a series of thoughts and feelings we have not been aware of. Let me give you an example of how petty irritations end up changing our mood from happy to morose.

Real-Life Example of Mood Change

Years ago when I worked in a small town, the commute time from home to the power station where I worked was only about ten minutes.

One day I left the office at 4:00 p.m. in a happy mood because I was expecting to join my tennis buddies on court at 4:30 p.m. However, by the time I reached home at 4:10 p.m., my mood had changed to one of anger and brooding.

I asked myself, "Why did my mood change from happy to angry all within the space of just ten minutes?" I retraced the incidents that had happened on my very short trip from my place of work.

First, as I reversed slowly from my garage, I was forced to apply the emergency brakes because another car just whizzed by without warning. Then when I reached the main gate, I had to queue behind a row of cars. When I was finally outside the gate and turning into the main road, a motorbike suddenly roared across the front of my car, again causing me to brake and so on.

By the time I reached home, at least ten petty disturbances (traffic-related and others) had impinged on my mind, thereby causing the appropriate negative feelings. I had not been consciously aware of my thoughts or feelings, but each petty incident had registered some irritation on my mind so that by the time I reached home I was in a real bad mood. In that state of mind any remark by my wife would have caused me to snap angrily and may have escalated into an argument. Later both of us would be left wondering what it was all about.

If I had been consciously aware of each incident and the feelings associated with it, then I would not have ended up being in such a foul mood! Thus, the first secret to maintaining happiness within us is to be aware of our feelings and thoughts at every instant.

If we can continually monitor our thoughts and feelings on an instant-by-instant basis and choose to change our thoughts to more happy ones, then we can cultivate the habit of happiness!

As I have mentioned early on in this book, our happiness depends on the thoughts we allow to occupy our minds. In order to ensure that these thoughts remain happy, we have to continually weed out the unhappy thoughts. To do that, we have to be aware of the state of our minds at every instant.

Our states of mind manifest in different ways in our behavior. If we are happy or unhappy, we behave differently, and this gives rise to certain external symptoms. So if we can observe our symptoms, we will know when we are unhappy inside. Then we can take steps to return to a happy state of mind. Below are a few common symptoms (some taken from my own experiences) that let us know when we are feeling unhappy inside.

Symptoms of Inner Unhappiness

1. *Being argumentative.* I used to always want to win an argument—even about the most trivial things. I wanted to be right all the time. This showed that I had not learned to accept myself, was not happy with my self-image, and needed to prove my superiority by being right. Nowadays after I have applied some of the principles in this book, I find that I have changed. In fact, an old friend of mine commented on this in surprise: "Gopi, you don't argue anymore!" Once I had accepted myself (warts and all), there was no more need to prove myself to others. I could still disagree, but without wanting the other person to agree with my views. I would just state my viewpoint and leave it up to the other to take it or leave it. How stress-free and relaxing is it to be able to do that!

2. *Being cynical.* This is a symptom that I do not suffer from because I have always had a trusting and positive outlook. However, a cynic is bound to be very unhappy inside. He doubts the sincerity of everyone, and he believes that every politician is bad, that the country is going to the dogs, that the

crime rate will only increase, and so on! How can he be happy with such an attitude when all he expects is the worst? Worse, when he focuses on such thoughts, then he is bound to attract unhappy experiences as a self-fulfilling prophecy. As someone once said, "It is all right to be skeptical as long as you are not cynical!"

3. *Always criticizing.* I used to have this problem, thinking I would have done it differently and better. I used to criticize everything and everyone to anyone who would listen. In fact, my wife stopped watching movies with me because I was incessantly criticizing the story, the director, the actors, the music, the cinematography, and so on. Now I realize that this is yet another symptom of unhappiness and poor self-image. I was trying to impress people by showing up the faults or mistakes of others. Nowadays I think I am much improved since my self-image is also better, and I have learned self-acceptance, especially after carrying out the mirror exercise (which is one of the happy living tips described in a later chapter).

4. *Reacting angrily instead of responding calmly.* If I have a negative judgment about another person, then everything he or she does is bound to annoy me! So I will react angrily to some small oversight or carelessness on the part of a family member or the maid or a colleague and so on.

   I finally realized that I was reacting not to their actions but to my own inner judgment of them. Because if the same oversight had been committed by someone I looked up to, then I would not react angrily but might even try to excuse the behavior!

   So I stopped judging people (as much as I could since this is an ongoing process) and found that the same actions that used to make me blow my top now did not even ruffle me. I was not only responding calmly but even looking indulgently at the behavior as being a unique and inherent part of that person the same way as we often look indulgently at the mischievous behavior of our own children!

5. *Always complaining.* This is different from item 3 (criticizing) in that complaining has no merit whatsoever while criticism can sometimes be constructive. Fortunately I am not much of a complainer, but a vast majority of people are. These are the ones who complain about their ill health, about crooked politicians, about the maid, about the boss, about the neighbors, about their own friends, and about everything under the sun!

If we look at our own behavior and notice that we are guilty of exhibiting any of these symptoms (such as constantly arguing, complaining, criticizing, being cynical, and reacting angrily rather than responding calmly), then we can be sure that we are unhappy inside.

Of course, there are many other symptoms of our inner unhappiness. But being aware of these few will already help us increase the happiness in our lives.

So what can we do to remove the inner unhappiness? How can we create happiness within?

We can remember to be aware of our feelings at each moment and the associated thoughts that bring about those feelings.

Once we are aware that we are judgmental of someone, then we can easily stop the judging attitude and practice acceptance of the other just as he or she is.

Once we are aware that it is our own lack of self-esteem that causes us to behave in certain unproductive ways, then we can take steps to improve our self-image by self-acceptance, by using the mirror exercise and other happy living tips, and especially by taking control of our thoughts!

Another way is to 'change channels', a technique described in chapter 14 under Happy Living Tip #3.

Truth #3: We Are All Programmed for Joy and Motivated by the Desire for Happiness

This has been mentioned briefly in chapter 2 under the title "Why Do We Humans Seek Happiness?" but I would like to go into greater detail here. (This point is so vital to the crux of the happy living philosophy that I feel some repetition is necessary and unavoidable in the following discussion.)

Just what is our *primary motivation* that makes us carry out any action? Is it money, love, greed, revenge, compassion, or fame? Actually it is none of these!

There is one basic motivation that prompts us to take any action. We just want to feel good! Sometimes even thinking that we will feel good is enough motivation to carry out a certain action.

Granted, one person's idea of feeling good may be totally different from another. (Some may even seem totally perverse.) But everyone acts in a way to feel good or think that it will make them feel good. Just think of all the various ways in which we act:

- Some people enjoy eating at roadside stalls, while others prefer to eat at expensive restaurants.
- Some prefer to spend lavishly, while others do the exact opposite and hoard their money.
- Some drink alcohol, and others are teetotalers.
- Some are vegetarians, while others cannot do without meat.

So although the actions may seem opposite, the reason or motivating force behind their actions is always the same. They want the feel-good emotion of happiness.

Sometimes people do things that may seem to be the exact opposite of feeling good. Take smoking for example. I dare say that no one really enjoyed their first puff! Their body would have rejected smoke going into their lungs by coughing and choking.

But they thought it would make them appear cool among their peers, and so they persevered. Our bodies are very adaptable, and so after some time it accepted the alien smoke and finally got addicted to it. Now the body needs the smoke to feel good! Thus, even the smoker is smoking to feel good.

- Why was Mother Theresa involved in charity work? Because it made her feel good. For her it was far better than getting married and raising a family, which would have made many other women very happy.

- Why do men buy expensive sports cars? They feel good because it is a symbol of prestige among the masses. If it was for pure speed, they could have attained that at a much cheaper price by buying a small car with a highly modified engine.

- Why do the women wear expensive jewelry or buy accessories and just keep them in a safe deposit box? They feel good when they wear it or even when they think that others will be impressed.

- Why do teenagers have body piercings and tattoos? To feel good thinking it is cool to do as their peers do.

- Why do we watch movies (whether horror, musical, comedy, or action movies)? We do it for the excitement, the entertainment—to feel good.

- Why do martyrs give up their lives for a belief? They expect to feel good in the hereafter.

- In public speaking, the applause makes the speaker feel good. Music, novels, and theater can provide intellectual happiness.

- Why do suicide bombers set off bombs killing innocent civilians? Because they believe that by sacrificing their lives here, they will be happy (feel good) in the afterlife!

- Why do failed lovers commit suicide? They don't feel good without the other. When people commit suicide, they are overriding their primary instinct of survival. Therefore, the desire for happiness even outweighs the survival instinct!

- Bungee jumping, mountain climbing, or skydiving—all done so that one can feel good!

In every instance mentioned above the primary motivation is always the same—to feel good! Now why should that be our primary motivation? That is so because it has been built into our system by the Creator. That is why I have been repeatedly saying, "We have been programmed for happiness! GOD wants us to be happy!"

That is also why Aristotle said two thousand years ago, "Happiness is the meaning and the purpose of life, the whole aim and end of human existence."

Now that brings us to the point where you ask, "Assuming we are all programmed for happiness, how can we go about attaining happiness?"

This whole book is written with the purpose of answering that question.

However, as a start I would like to introduce the ultimate commandments. I sincerely believe that there are only three ultimate commandments that we need to follow to lead a happy and fulfilled life here on earth and also in the hereafter!

What then are these three ultimate commandments? First let me tell you what they are *not*.

- It is not about forbidding something or other.
- It is not about honor or duty or the like.
- It is not about sinning or salvation and so on.
- It is not about avoiding the wrath of God.
- It is not about using the name of God in vain.

In fact, the three ultimate commandments cannot be found in the ubiquitous Ten Commandments! So then you ask, "How can the ultimate commandments not be found within the Ten Commandments, which millions have believed in for ages? How can it not have anything to do with not stealing, not killing, not coveting, honor, or duty?

And I will answer, "Sadly this is the where most of us go wrong by our blind belief in things said or written long ago by people long gone— not having enough confidence in our own individual GOD-given mind-brain combination to think rationally; always giving up our right to question, and instead lazily accepting blindly anything that is put before us, whether it has merit or not!

If we are open to reason, then we may be able to clear away the cobwebs that have shrouded the minds of men and women since time immemorial. So, now I am going to ask you to join me in finding out exactly what the ultimate commandments are. We are going to be led to the answer by means of questions which we can rationally ask and answer. This will lead us to the truth without any deceptions.

Let me ask you first of all, "What one thing does every one of us human beings want?" What do we want so badly that we may prefer to die if we do not have it? What are we programmed for?

In one word the answer is happiness! Yes, we are all programmed from birth for happiness!

I can say this with conviction because I know there is not one person among the billions who has ever prayed for unhappiness! No one prays as follows, "God give me some sorrow! I am too happy in this world! I would like to be sad for a while."

Why not? We have not done so because we are programmed by our Creator only for happiness and not for misery.

Then you ask, "If that is true, then why is there so much unhappiness in the world?"

Mainly because we have not understood this primary requirement—that we are created in this wonderful world to be happy! Instead, many of us have been taught that it is not right or even possible to be happy in the now. Many of us have also been told we have a right to be happy only in the hereafter. Some preach to us that we are born sinners and we are here to do penance and pray for forgiveness. Others say that we are here only to work out our bad karma in a previous life. The gist of these teachings being that we are born on earth to suffer, not to be happy!

However, let me say it clearly once and for all: GOD wants us to be happy! GOD wants us to be happy here on earth and in the hereafter! In fact, GOD has so created this world and programmed our minds so that we can all achieve this state of happiness now. By achieving happiness here and now, we can also be happy in the hereafter.

Now let me clarify a few things about what real happiness is.

Real happiness is all about empathy, desire, growth, achievement, and so on—all positive values. Real happiness is expansive and not contracting. It is inclusive and does not exclude.

Happiness is not about greed, selfishness, lust, and so on. That is what I call pseudo happiness. So we can also call real happiness joy. I remember that someone once said, "You are not just a human being but a human becoming." What I guess he or she meant is that each of us is an evolving human being.

Part of the process of self-evolution is making the most of our talents and going after our desires with our whole heart and whole soul so that in the process we grow, evolve, and become better persons.

It is to help us achieve this that the Creator has hardwired into our DNA the following primary imperatives, which I call the ultimate commandments:

1. Thou shall be happy (or joyful).
2. Thou shall spread happiness (joy).
3. Thou shall preserve and protect your joy.

That's it! That's all! You don't need to go about forbidding this, that, and the other; forbidding never works. Saying, "Don't," always seems to have the opposite result. Let me give you a simple example.

The Fence with the Knotholes

Let us say that every day on your way to work you pass by a seven-foot-high fence made of planks and that there is a knothole on two of the planks. You have been walking by the same fence every day for more than a year. Never once did you feel the urge to peep through one of the knotholes.

Now today you notice that someone has printed the words, "Don't peep," below one of the knotholes.

What happens? You suddenly get the urge to take a look just because it has been forbidden. And it would take a lot of self-control to avoid peeping. Let us take it a step further. The next day you find the words, "Please peep," below the second knothole.

My question is this: Which knothole tempts you to take a peep? The one that says, "Please peep," or the one that says, "Don't peep"? The vast majority of us, I dare say, will feel tempted by the forbidden rather than the permitted.

That is why I believe that forbidding never works. We humans seem to be built that way. We want to explore what is challenging and forbidden rather than things that are easy and allowed. Anyone who has raised children will know the above statement to be only too true!

Note that perhaps it is because most of the Ten Commandments begin with "Thou shall not—" that people seem to be constantly breaking those commandments. As you well know, our minds are not able to work with a negative command. For example, if I were to say, "Don't think of a yellow flying snake," you can't help visualizing one. This is also why it is not possible to get out of poverty by saying, "I don't want to be poor." The mind focuses on the word 'poor' and not on the word 'don't'. Hence, we get more chances to remain poor! Similarly if we say, "I don't want to be sick," we are more likely to remain sick than if we say, "I am healthy."

Now it is time to look at these three commandments one by one.

1. **Thou Shall Be Joyful!**

   Why? Because being joyful is the purpose of your life. It is simply crazy to think that the Creator took so much trouble to create such a complex and wonderful world and gave us such incredible potential just so that GOD could watch us suffer and gloat at our misery.

   Only a sick mind could have conceived of such an idea, but the strange thing is that many millions of people have been programmed, conditioned, and brainwashed to believe such things. Some believe that GOD sent us to Earth as punishment, that life on earth is a curse we have to endure to work out our karma, and that life on earth is an illusion and therefore unimportant.

The absolute truth is that if you are happy, you naturally spread this happiness to your spouse, your children, and your family as well as your work colleagues.

If you are happy inside, you are slow to anger and quick to forgive. A happy person does not instigate fights or start wars.

So it makes total sense for you to go after your own happiness.

Thus, a happy person automatically spreads joy, which leads nicely into the next commandment.

2. **Thou Shall Spread Joy!**

Why? Simply because this one commandment will help you ensure that your actions when they relate to others are always aligned with joy! Just ask yourself the following questions:

- When you are unfaithful to your spouse, do you spread joy?
- When you steal from another, do you spread joy?
- When you kill someone, do you spread joy?
- When you covet your neighbor's goods, do you spread joy?
- When you covet your neighbor's wife, do you spread joy?
- When you use God's name in vain, do you spread joy?
- When you bear false witness against your neighbor, do you spread joy?

The answer to all the above questions is a resounding no! Of course not! On the other hand, do you spread joy by honoring your parents? Of course you do! So the existing commandments are all geared to this one idea of spreading joy! I could add a few other examples, such as these: When you are angry, do you spread joy? When you hurt another, do you spread joy?

Thus, this one commandment of spreading joy covers every one of the existing commandments and more (except the ones that are set up by the religious authorities to ensure their own survival, which I do not wish to delve into).

Now how can we spread joy? We can spread joy by asking ourselves, "Does this action spread joy?" Then we can go ahead with it. If it will not spread joy but instead add to the misery of the world, then we can refrain from taking that action.

We can only spread joy when first we are happy ourselves, and then we want to see others happy! That is why we automatically feel happy when we help another person.

3. **Thou Shall Preserve Joy!**

Why? I believe this commandment is necessary just as self-defense is necessary when our lives are threatened. In case our joy is threatened, we have a few options if we wish to preserve it.

- We can avoid the person or place that is causing us to lose our joy.
- We can apply the relevant happy living tip/tips to respond appropriately so as to defuse the situation.
- In extreme cases such as physical attacks on our person or on our family members, then we have to defend ourselves to the best of our ability in order to preserve our joy, even if it means going against the second commandment (about spreading joy).

*   *   *

So that is Truth #3 about happiness: "We are all programmed by GOD for joy and we are also motivated by the desire for happiness."

Therefore, it should not be that much of a problem for us to make happy living a way of life since we are already programmed for happiness and we are motivated by happiness! All we need is to change our belief systems so that we are in alignment with what GOD and nature intended for us.

Truth #4: Happiness Can Be Enhanced with Happiness Enhancers!

Happiness enhancers can be considered the second phase of happy living. The first phase of happy living is to learn to make happiness a habit, no matter what the external circumstances. Once we already know how to be happy in spite of circumstances, then and only then are we ready to use happiness enhancers to change our circumstances for the better.

The fact remains that happiness is mainly a state of mind where the mind includes the intellect as well as feelings/emotions. (I am not separating the head and heart in the conventional way as mentioned earlier in chapter 1.) And the state of the mind depends on the thoughts we focus on. Thus, by focusing on happy thoughts we can create a happy, peaceful state of mind!

Then and only then can we truly enjoy or appreciate the external pleasures. If we are not happy or at peace within us, external or sensory pleasures alone will not make us happy. For example, if there has been a death in the family, can we enjoy our favorite food, drink, music, or even company? Of course not!

But if we were already in a happy state of mind (say we passed an exam with flying colors or got a promotion we had been wanting), then we can really enjoy all the external pleasures. These external pleasures are what I call happiness enhancers, which should be pursued with passion but not obsession!

What then is a happiness enhancer? A happiness enhancer is anything that increases or intensifies the happiness we already feel.

It can only increase the happiness that you already have. If you are unhappy in mind, then it cannot be of much help. A happiness enhancer can be any of a thousand different things and vary from person to person. An example will clarify this better.

Let us take the case of a small family consisting of a father, mother, and three children. They have a comfortable income, and they communicate well with each other and can be considered to be a happy family. One day while they are watching the Travel Channel, the children are excited at seeing Disneyland.

The parents then decide that they want to take the kids to Disneyland. It becomes one of their goals! So they excitedly plan, save some money, and in due course of time take the kids on a holiday to Disneyland!

That is an example of a happiness enhancer. The goal or purpose of letting the kids enjoy Disneyland gives the parents new motivation, new excitement, and new enthusiasm.

It is not that the family was unhappy to start with. They were already happy. Not making the trip to Disneyland would not make them unhappy, but going on the holiday would enhance or increase their happiness by giving them new adventures, experiences, and memories.

Happiness enhancers can vary from person to person, but generally they are anything that can make one feel good. Examples can include the following:

- money
- having a purpose in life and knowing that purpose
- good health
- possessions
- friendships
- success in career or business
- reciprocated love
- good food and drinks
- community service
- achievement of our dreams and goals
- playing or listening to music
- winning a competition
- dancing
- conversation

Now let's elaborate on a few major examples.

Money: This is one of the most powerful of happiness enhancers. Money has the power to create whatever we can think of on the physical plane. It can build houses, schools, and factories. It can buy cars, jewelry, food, and holidays. It can do charitable work. It can send up satellites. It can help the sick and so on.

Purpose: This is another very fulfilling happiness enhancer. This is what drives the inventor, the entrepreneur, the athlete, the community worker, and so on. Without purpose you have no will to live. That is why many retirees decline and die soon after they stop working. They have nothing to look forward to—only death! If they have new hobbies or other things, such as an online blog or a new activity (music, dancing, gardening, or travel) to keep them occupied, then their happiness would be enhanced.

Health: Being healthy and fit can enhance your happiness and help you enjoy life! In fact, this is one of the best happiness enhancers. However, the reason I placed money at the top of the list is purely for practicality.

Everyone knows that good health is a prime factor for happiness. However, that alone does not motivate us to strive for good health! Most of us only wish for good health but are not motivated to become healthy. We avoid going to the gym. We eat unhealthily.

It is only when we get sick that we become really motivated to try to remedy the situation. This means going to doctors, healers, and so on, which again needs money. So in the real world people go first after money followed by life purpose, and then they think about health.

Because each person is unique, there are innumerable happiness enhancers. For example, consider the following:

- Edison found happiness in invention.
- Donald Trump finds happiness in real estate.

- Lincoln found his happiness in giving justice and equality to his people.
- Bill Gates finds happiness in his charities.
- Branson finds happiness in maverick businesses.
- Hefner finds happiness in bringing sex out of the closet.
- Ferrari finds happiness in making superlative cars.
- Jay Leno finds happiness in buying cars.

Unfortunately most people think that these things (by themselves) are what will make them truly happy. They do not realize that these are only happiness enhancers and that true happiness is firstly of the mind. Many people are frustrated with life because they go after the happiness enhancers only without first attaining peace of mind.

Happiness enhancers are vital if we are to live fulfilled lives. They are what will give us the motivation to go after our dreams and goals confidently. Happiness enhancers give us short-term purposes for our existence. They also help us avoid boredom, which is one of the unhappiest states to be in.

The only caveat in pursuing any or all of these happiness enhancers is to do it in balance—don't be obsessed with any one thing. The one who is obsessed with food becomes a glutton. The one obsessed with money becomes cold and calculating. The one obsessed with power becomes a megalomaniac and so on.

Being obsessed is not a happy place to be. In fact, it is the closest to hell you can experience on earth! We must remember that happiness is of the senses, of the mind, and of the soul. These must be in balance. Going after any one of these to the exclusion of the others will lead to unhappiness.

I would like to bring this chapter to a close with a wonderful quote from the *Science of Getting Rich* by Wallace D Wattles. Following are excerpts from chapter 5 entitled Increasing Life:

> *The Universe desires you to have everything you want to have. Nature is friendly to your plans. Everything is naturally for you. Make up your mind that this is true!*
>
> *Life is the performance of function and the individual really lives only when he performs every function—physical, mental, and spiritual—of which he is capable without excess in any!*
>
> *You do not want to get rich solely for the gratification of animal desires. That is not life. But the performance of every physical function is a part of life, and no one lives completely who denies the impulses of the body.*
>
> *You do not want to get rich solely to enjoy mental pleasures, to get knowledge, to gratify ambition, to outshine others, to be famous. All these are a legitimate part of life, but the person who lives for the pleasures of the intellect alone will only have a partial life.*
>
> *You do not want to get rich solely for the good of others, to lose yourself in the salvation of mankind, to experience the joys of philanthropy and sacrifice. The joys of the soul are only a part of life, and they are no better or nobler than any other part.*
>
> *You want to get rich in order that you may eat, drink and be merry when it is time to do those things; in order that you may surround yourself with beautiful things, see*

distant lands, feed your mind, and develop your intellect; in order that you may love others and do kind things, and be able to play a good part in helping the world to find truth.

PART 4

Practical Application of the Joycentrix Principles

Now at last we come to the most important part of this book—the practical application of the Joycentrix principles. All that has gone before was mere theory.

In school the study of a theorem in geometry or a law in physics and chemistry consisted only of the introduction and needed us to work out a lot of problems or exercises so as to really understand and assimilate the theory.

Similarly in life, we need to test out and experiment with the happy living principles in actual practical cases before we can truly understand and apply them. Part 4 of this book is devoted to just this ideal.

So here we go! Get ready to put yourself in the place of the examples given so that you really begin to experience what we have been talking about in parts 1, 2, and 3.

Be prepared to acquire new, more useful beliefs that will help you achieve happiness to replace all those self-defeating beliefs that only give you unhappiness.

CHAPTER 13

Introduction to Happy Living Tips

Over the past several chapters we have explored a number of principles of happy living. From here onward we will see how to put these principles into practice in our daily lives.

As I have said before it is our deep-seated beliefs that create our reality. Whether our lives are happy or miserable, whether we are successful achievers or failures, whether we have happy relationships or not, whether we are paranoid or at peace with the world, everything depends on how we habitually think and what beliefs we hold.

Thus, the principles of happy living I'm talking about are no more than beliefs that we choose to accept. We choose these beliefs because it makes sense to us and will enable us to achieve daily happy living.

Best of all, we do have the power to choose our beliefs. So why not choose self-empowering rather than self-defeating beliefs?

In order to do this, I have provided **more than a dozen happy living tips** based on the principles of the Joycentrix System.

These tips are what I have been using and still use to keep myself happy every day in spite of challenging circumstances that are part of daily life. Tip #1 about Creating a Happiness Aura has already been described earlier in chapter ten.

In the chapters that follow I shall describe how to use each of these separately or in combination to solve some common challenges encountered in life like the following:

- Attaining Equanimity and Peace of Mind
- Having Happier Relationships
- Learning to Be Grateful for Life
- How to Feel Upbeat and Energized
- Dealing with People

CHAPTER 14

Attaining Equanimity and Peace of Mind

When we speak of being happy, the first thing we need to attain is equanimity (i.e., a state of mind when we are calm and imperturbable). We feel at peace, and we are not easily disturbed by people or circumstances. Even on those few occasions when we feel rattled by something or someone, we are able to quickly come back to an even keel and retain our equanimity.

The following happy living tips #2 and #3 will help us to attain some form of equanimity, even though perfect equanimity may be impossible for most of us.

Happy Living Tip #2: Starting the Day Right

This is a specific, practical, and simple tip that will help you start your day right. Don't overlook this tip or underestimate its usefulness just because it seems so simple and trite!

*First thing in the morning, greet someone at home with a
bright, cheery, and enthusiastic, "Good morning!"*

Living alone? Then as soon as you wake up, look at yourself in the
mirror and say, "Good morning," to yourself with all the cheerfulness
and enthusiasm you can muster.

It is important you do this first thing in the morning so that you start
the day right. Do not wait until you reach your office to wish your
office colleagues. By the time you reach the office, the traffic might
have put you in a despondent mood.

Now you may be thinking, how can such a simple action help me
become happy? The reason is that there are several underlying principles
involved in carrying out that simple action. These are listed below.

Underlying Principles

- *Happy thoughts lead to cheerful actions.* To sound enthusiastic,
  you need to feel cheerful. To feel cheerful, you need to think
  happy thoughts. This is one of the principles at work here.

- *When we feel happy, we send out good vibrations.* I am sure
  each one of you has experienced this principle. At a party
  some people repel you, and some attract you. Do you think
  it is the miserable ones who attract you? (If so, you need to
  be aware of this principle all the more and do some serious
  soul-searching.)

- *We speak it into existence.* This is allied to your belief and the
  law of attraction. If you expect a good morning, you are much

more likely to enjoy one. What kind of day can you expect if you say, "What a lousy day"?

Practical Application

The first thing I do when I wake up is to be grateful for waking up! As some wit once said, "Anytime you wake up without a chalk outline around your body, it's a great day!"

Then to put myself in a good mood I look out the window and truly appreciate what I see and what I hear. I realize how grateful I am that I am able to see, I am able to hear, I can walk, I can talk, and so on. How wonderful it is to be alive!

On days when I wake up and feel lousy, I talk to myself as follows:

> Question: "Why am I feeling lousy at this moment?"

> Answer: *I'm feeling bad because I'm thinking some lousy thoughts.*

> Q: "Gopi, who is in control of your thoughts?"

> A: *I am.*

> Q: "So why not choose to think only thoughts that will make you feel good?"

Why not indeed? Then I deliberately think happy thoughts. The easiest way to do that is to feel grateful for things I do have and to use Happy Living Tip #3 (Change Channels). Within a few minutes I am feeling good and upbeat. Then I am in the mood to go downstairs and greet my wife with a bright and cheery "Good morning!"

Since I began this practice several years ago, both my wife and I have actually come to look forward to our morning greetings. We even try to outdo each other to see who sounds more enthusiastic! This is really a far cry from all those days of glum greetings or no greetings at all.

Well, Friends, just try it! Say, "Good morning," enthusiastically to yourself or your spouse or your colleagues and see how your day brightens up for you.

Happy Living Tip #3: Changing Channels Technique

Happy Living Tip #3 is all about what I call "changing channels technique."

I find it extremely effective in helping me keep a happy frame of mind. It is a simple seventeen-second technique taught by Dr. Robert Anthony, a popular author and self-help guru. I learned this several years ago when I studied one of his courses. I use it regularly, and you may want to do so too—if you want to remain cheerful.

Dr. Robert Anthony calls it the "flip switch technique," but I prefer to call it "change channels" because it relates easier to me since I watch TV a lot. When I don't like a particular program or even a segment of the program, I immediately change channels to one that I do like (much to my wife's chagrin)! She dislikes switching between channels and would prefer to remain on one channel even if it was boring.

To come back to the matter at hand, I have mentioned before that we have to be aware of our thoughts and feelings from instant to instant and choose the thoughts we allow to dwell in our mind. Nice word . . . *dwell*, which means to stay in a place (dwelling). Just as we would be careful to vet the tenants who dwell in our apartments or houses, so should we also vet the thoughts that we allow to reside in our minds!

Happy Living Tip #3 helps us do just that. According to Dr. Robert Anthony:

> *"Whenever you become aware that you are not in a happy mood, change your thoughts instantly by thinking of something pleasant and holding that pleasant thought for seventeen seconds."*

When you are able to hold the new happier thought for more than seventeen seconds, the older unhappy thought is displaced, and you will start to feel happier!

Underlying Principles

Our thoughts create our moods or emotions. Hence, if we take care to replace our thoughts at every instant to those that are more in harmony with what we really want (i.e., to feel good), then we can gradually make it a habit to be happy. When we feel happy, we send out good vibrations, so we attract good things into our lives.

Dr. Robert Anthony says, "No one is going to flow positive energy all day long. Flip switching is simply an action you take to get from a low vibration, to a higher one."

Practical Application

There are many ways to 'flip switch' or 'change channels', but I favor the following:

- *Look at photos of loved ones.* I keep a special photo album of my sons with pictures from when they were small. Whenever I look at those endearing, funny, or silly photos, my mood changes immediately to one of happiness. Initially when I was practicing this tip, I kept the small album handy, and every time I needed to change channels, I looked at these photos. After some time these photos were so ingrained in my mind that I only had to think about the photos and I would feel happy. So I could easily change channels in my mind! (Nowadays I have photos and videos of my grandchildren to look at!)

  There is a caveat about loved ones. It is preferable to think about small children because most parents feel unconditional love for them. It may not work as well with your teenager, spouse, or significant other, especially if your unhappy feelings started because of them!

- *Think of your pets.* If you are single, then you can do the same as above with photos of your pets!

- *Think of past successes.* List your past successes and achievements that mean a lot to you and read them often. When you want to use these happy thoughts and feelings associated with them, it can become easy and habitual.

- *Think of lovely travel destinations.* If you have photos of any favorite cities, sceneries, or sunsets that give you serenity and peace and joy, then you can use them as described above for loved ones.

Therefore, whenever you feel out of sorts or unhappy, monitor your thoughts at that instant and immediately think of happier thoughts for about seventeen seconds or so until you become happier.

The above technique works because of another unchangeable law of the mind that says, "We can only hold one thought uppermost in our mind at any one time. When we focus on another thought, the new thought automatically displaces the earlier thought!"

Although some may argue that it is possible for many people to multitask, I submit that it is not the same thing. In so-called multitasking (such as talking on the phone when driving or watching TV while feeding the baby), most of the tasks are habitual. You do not have to think about driving when you drive. You do it automatically.

This is not the same as using your mind to think two different things at the same time. I challenge any person of normal ability to write a letter answering a customer's complaint while at the same time applying for a visa online. For any ordinary person it is just not possible to hold two separate trains of thoughts at the same time.

Word of Caution

Even though we may be regularly following happy living tips 2 and 3, there may be times when we do slip up. Therefore, we still need to be on guard all the time. Let me give you my own experience recently.

One day last week I started off the day as usual by putting myself in a happy frame of mind and wished my wife a bright and cheery "Good morning" and had a great breakfast. Then I sat down to read the newspaper.

About half an hour later when I had finished the paper, I found that I was not in a good mood anymore! What had happened? As I read each news item (the snatch theft, the armed robbery, the scandal, the rape and the abuse of children, etc.), it had an impact on my mind. Although consciously unaware, I was thinking about each item of morbid news, and this in turn caused my feelings to reflect the negative thoughts, which is why I ended up being in a bad mood.

So now I make it a point **not** to read the main newspaper first. Instead, I read the lifestyle, entertainment, and sports pages or even the classifieds. Even if I do glance at some political news, I make sure I am constantly aware of my feelings. If reading any item makes me feel angry, vengeful, or helpless, I immediately stop reading that item.

Personally I have totally stopped reading about child abuse cases because it affects me very badly. My wife helps by warning me to avoid page 11 or 13 if those pages contain any such news. This brings up another question. Why is my wife not affected by the news?

My wife wants and needs to read the newspaper every day! She says she just wants to know what is going on in the world, and she doesn't brood about the news as I do. So she says it is okay for her. Perhaps she is right to some extent. I notice that she never cries at movies because she is unable to identify with the characters. So maybe she is able to look at news items as something out there and not relate to it personally!

However, when it comes to funerals of family and friends, she tends to gets overly emotional. She is also affected by a snatch theft in our neighborhood and can be heard intently discussing it with her friends on the phone. This leaves her feeling worried about going out for a walk, opening the house gate, and so on. So in spite of her protests to the contrary, no one (not even my wife) is immune from this immutable law of the mind. When we think certain thoughts, we attract similar thoughts!

This is very easily proven. In any group, say if you were to start a topic about weddings, others will also start talking of weddings, and the atmosphere will generally be one of celebration and cheer. If you were to switch topics to funerals, all at once others will think about funerals, and a sudden pall will come over the group. Again, if you switch topics once more and talk of ghost stories, immediately there will be others contributing their own ghost stories!

We just can't help it! That is how we are created. There is no running away from this law of the mind. What you think about attracts like thoughts, and since your thoughts determine your feelings, what thoughts you focus on determine your mood! Hence, if you constantly monitor your thoughts and feelings and keep choosing the happy ones, then you can remain happy!

In order to choose our thoughts and our feelings, we have to be aware of them from instant to instant. If we are aware that we are not feeling happy in the moment, then we can take steps to identify the thoughts that gave rise to that feeling and change them as necessary.

In this chapter we have learned how to attain some form of peace of mind and equanimity by applying the two simple happy living tips #2 and #3.

CHAPTER 15

Having Happier Relationships

B eing nonjudgmental is the best prescription for happy relationships between husband and wife, between colleagues, and between friends. In order not to judge others, we need to learn self-acceptance as well as the acceptance of others. We also need to be able to forgive ourselves and others. The happy living tips that I use and would recommend for improving our day-to-day relationships with others are tips #4 and #5. These are described in this chapter.

Happy Living Tip #4: The Mirror Exercise

This is a tip that will help establish happy relationships between you and your spouse, your friends, your colleagues, and all other people.

All you do is look at yourself in the mirror with love twice every day for about five minutes at a time!

I can hear you readers going, "I look at myself in the mirror every day so what is the difference?" The difference is that I am not talking about looking at the external you as you do when you are brushing your teeth or washing your face or shaving or putting on makeup! You are to practice looking at yourself (the complete you) with love!

Initial Challenges

Initially when I first started the mirror exercise, my mind could only focus on things that I did not like about myself, namely my imperfections—nose too big, crooked teeth, balding, and so on. So how could I love myself? (Most probably you, too, may have similar negative feelings at first.)

But after persisting for several days, one day I suddenly realized that *I was much more than the external me.* I said to myself, "Hey, with all my imperfections, I am still special. I am lovable. I am one of a kind. I deserve to love and be loved. I am so much more than my looks! I am a unique soul with so much to offer to the world."

Imagine if someone invented a doll that could raise its eyebrows or smile or cry or frown. Wouldn't we consider that doll to be special? But we are able to do much more than that. We can not only do all the above but can also think (imagine, dream, plan), feel emotions (happiness, anger, sorrow, generosity, compassion, altruism), and so on.

When we realize just how special and unique we are in spite of our imperfections, then we attain the state of unconditional love! This state of loving yourself unconditionally is called self-acceptance.

Self-Acceptance

The first step in achieving happy human relationships is self-acceptance. If we cannot love ourselves, how can others love us? Also if we cannot love ourselves, how can we love others?

I once heard someone say insightfully: "The problem with going for a holiday is that I have to take myself!" How true? If we cannot find peace within ourselves, it makes no difference which country or holiday resort we go to. We still won't find peace and happiness.

So the first thing is that you must accept yourself with all your good and bad points—your talents and your faults, your strengths and your weaknesses, your quirks and your foibles! Then you will be able to accept others just as they are, which is the second step in maintaining happy human relationships.

Acceptance of Others

This will automatically follow from self-acceptance. Once you can accept and love yourself, then you can accept others just as they are without trying to change them!

This is the key to all happy relationships—accepting your spouse or children or friends for what they are and not for what you want them to be! Most marital relationships collapse because one spouse is always trying to change the other to his or her own ideal concept. Since each one of us has our own ego, we don't like it when others try to change us. We feel that it reflects badly on our own image. That is why none of us like to be nagged at.

When you accept yourself, then you are able to respect and love yourself! If you love and respect yourself, then you become more confident, and you are less sensitive to slights (whether imagined or real) and do not react inappropriately but respond reasonably. Thus, you become easy to get along with, thereby making for happy human relationships.

Practical Application

1. Do the mirror exercise twice a day without fail as described above and really learn self-acceptance. If you persist, sooner or later you will learn to love yourself unconditionally.

2. When it comes to our spouse or child, look for the good in each one of them and not the faults! What we focus on expands. If we look for faults, we are guaranteed to find them. If we look for the good, we are also sure to find them. Then we can appreciate all the good and excuse or understand their weaknesses. Hence, there is no stress in the relationship.

So that is Happy Living Tip #4: Do the mirror exercise and learn self-acceptance and the acceptance of others. Try it for yourself for a couple of weeks and prepare to be surprised at your results.

> NOTE: You don't have to wait for the other to reciprocate. In fact, you should not even expect that, for that is the basis of acceptance. Even if only one spouse was to learn self-acceptance and be willing to accept the other, the relationship is bound to improve. The idea about needing two hands to clap does not apply here.

The next relevant tip for happy relationships is Happy Living Tip #5, which is discussed below.

* * *

Happy Living Tip #5: How to Forgive Someone

This is another important tip on happy living and has to do with forgiveness, specifically the practical aspects of forgiving. We have always heard people tell us that it is good to forgive, but we are not given any specific details on how to forgive.

That is what this tip is all about. We will explore the practical aspects of forgiving others. To do this I have separated the people to be forgiven into two categories—"strangers and acquaintances" and "family and close friends." These are described below.

Part 1: Forgiving Strangers and Acquaintances

The first thing to realize about forgiveness is that you are not doing it for the other person but for yourself! Because when you think about the perceived injury to your ego or self-esteem, the feelings of anger, shame, and hurt are all within your own mind.

And you continue to feel insulted or shamed and get angry when you insist on dwelling on the injury in your own mind. Externally there may be nothing to show for the hurt you feel. The person who caused it may be gone for good, or you may not meet him or her again.

If you have been following along with the ideas in this book, you already know that your mind is completely under your own control.

You can choose what thoughts you allow to stay or change those thoughts as you like.

So how does it benefit you to keep thinking of the perceived injury again and again? You are only hurting yourself repeatedly by your continuing resentment. By continuing to think of tit-for-tat revenge to get back at the person involved, you are only poisoning your own physical system.

The excess adrenaline rush is in your body. The hormonal imbalance is in your body. The side effects of these are also going to show up in your own body and mind! You are not affecting the other person in any way at all. Once you realize this, it is easy to forgive the other person. By the act of forgiving, the one you help is really yourself and not the other!

Also the forgiving act you do is in your own mind! You do not have to go up to the other person and say, "I forgive you," or anything like that. Just say inside your own mind, "Bless you. Have a good life," or something to that effect and then close the book on the incident.

Here is a test to know if you have really forgiven: If you hear the other person's name mentioned and your mind does not immediately go back to that incident and if it does not affect you one way or another, then you have truly forgiven!

If you can think about that person without feeling upset or hurt or envious, then you have truly forgiven. On the other hand, if you carry with you any vestiges of the perceived injury, then the very mention of the person's name will bring about renewed feelings of frustration and anger.

For a firsthand example of how I managed to learn to forgive and forget, read "How I Overcame My Road Rage Almost Overnight" in chapter 12.

Part 2: Forgiving Family and Close Friends

It is easier to forgive strangers and acquaintances because we may not see them again or we may only see them again very rarely. Hence, there are less chances of being reminded about the hurt or anger.

However, with family members and close friends, it is quite different. We cannot avoid seeing them or interacting with them on a daily basis. Hence, the incident that caused the hurt or anger will keep coming back into our minds every time we see them.

Also our expectations for family and friends are higher. We expect them to understand us and feel for us much more so than we would expect from any others. So we end up feeling greater hurt and disappointment.

The key here is expectation. It is because we expect a certain behavior or a specific reaction from our family that we feel betrayed and are truly hurt when we don't get that behavior or reaction.

So the solution to this problem is unconditional acceptance and love! The word unconditional is very important when it comes to family. If we love and accept the family member unconditionally, then we find it easier to forgive him or her.

The first two steps in forgiving a family member are very similar to that for forgiving a stranger.

1. Remember that when we decide to forgive someone, we are actually thinking of ourselves (our own well-being) and not that of the other person! In a way it can be considered a selfish act—one that benefits us more.

2. Remember too that by nursing thoughts of anger and hurt within our own minds, we are poisoning our own selves physically (by the excess hormones we generate), mentally (by our thinking), and emotionally (by our negative feelings).

3. As an extra step when we are forgiving a member of the family or a close friend, we must learn to accept them unconditionally! If we are judgmental about our spouse or other family member, then we are bound to react to them based on our assumption of their motives. We will not be able to respond fairly to their actions because we will always be inferring ulterior motives to their actions.

The other thing is that when we hold some form of judgment about another person, we will be sending out different vibrations than those we would send if we love them totally unconditionally.

For example, if I think my wife is unsupportive, then whatever she says, does, or does not do (however innocently) will be viewed by me from the viewpoint of her being unsupportive. And it is easy to find fault from a judgmental perspective.

Thus, there is no way I can forgive her unless and until I practice being nonjudgmental and have unconditional acceptance of her! I have to see her as a good, loving person albeit with some faults or quirks, just as each one of us is with our own flaws and failings.

When I can come to this place of self-acceptance and acceptance of my spouse as perfect at her own level of evolution, then it will become much easier for me to forgive her when she upsets me by doing things that I do not expect.

When we begin to practice unconditional love and acceptance, we will experience less and less situations that upset or hurt us. When we begin to feel unconditional love for others, they can sense it, and they will automatically respond to those positive vibrations and will begin to act in ways to reciprocate our love and acceptance. Thus, they will often say or do things that please us and not upset us.

In this chapter we have covered two important tips for having happier relationships, namely Tip #4 (mirror exercise) and Tip #5 (how to forgive someone). In the next chapter we will explore some methods of learning to be grateful for life.

CHAPTER 16

Learning to Be Grateful for Life

Being grateful is one of the easiest and best ways for us to be happy on a daily basis. To help us in this quest I have provided two more happy living tips, namely Tip #6 and Tip #7.

Tip #6 is about starting a gratitude diary and is a wonderful suggestion for happy living. I know that at times it is very difficult to feel grateful when everything seems to be going wrong. But it is exactly when things don't seem to be going right that we have to exercise our gratitude muscles. Let's take the following worst-case scenario of a thirty-year-old male named Alex.

Alex's Worst Day

Alex has just arrived at his office late after he had struggled through one of the worst traffic jams. Then he gets the news that he has been retrenched!

He also receives a notice saying his car will be repossessed within fourteen days. Then there is a call from his credit card company politely reminding him that he is behind in the monthly payment.

He checks his e-mails, and there is a "Dear John" letter waiting from his longtime girlfriend, announcing that she is breaking up with him! What a day!

Now if at that time I were to tell Alex to count his blessings, he would be excused for trying to strangle me!

After he calms down, I would say to him:

"Alex, I know you have had a lousy day. But think about this for a minute. You can hear me when I talk, can't you? (You are not deaf.) You can see me. (You are not blind.) You can walk over to me and try to strangle me. (You are not crippled). Your mental faculties are intact, and you are also healthy, aren't you? So you are so much better off than the thousands or millions of people who are not as lucky as you!

"For all you know this retrenchment might be a fabulous chance for you to go after your dreams rather than struggle daily in a frustrating job. In a couple of months you would have settled all your outstanding bills and be looking forward to life! Perhaps you will meet your soul mate now that you are free of your old girlfriend.

"But all these can only happen if you are in a happy frame of mind. If you are in a dejected or depressed state and go about with a black cloud hanging over your head, you will not be able to see or grasp any new opportunities that can come up!

"Worrying and complaining will only make you feel worse, and you will attract a miserable future as a self-fulfilling prophecy! So when things seem to be at their worst that is often the best time to start thinking of things to be grateful for."

That realization is the basis of this happy living tip.

Happy Living Tip #6: Start a Daily Gratitude Diary!

Just get any exercise book, note today's date and start writing down at least five things you are grateful for today.

Underlying Principles

One of the best explanations I have read about gratitude and its power is by Wallace D. Wattles in his classic *The Science of Getting Rich* (SOGR), which was written about a century ago! He devotes the whole of chapter 7 to this topic of gratitude. Some of the highlights are given below:

There is a law of gratitude, and it is absolutely necessary that you should observe the law if you are to get the results you seek. It is the natural principle that action and reaction are always equal and in opposite directions. The grateful outreaching of your mind in thankful praise to the Supreme Intelligence is a liberation or expenditure of force. It cannot fail to reach that to which it is addressed and the reaction is an instantaneous movement towards you!

But the value of gratitude does not consist solely of getting you more blessings in the future. Without gratitude you cannot keep from dissatisfied thought regarding things as they are. To permit your mind to dwell on the inferior is to surround yourself with inferior things.

The grateful mind is constantly fixed on the best. Therefore it tends to become the best. It takes the character and form of the best and so will receive the best.

Also faith is born of gratitude. The grateful mind continually expects good things and expectation becomes faith. (Wallace D. Wattles)

Practical Application

When beginning the gratitude diary, initially you may struggle with it, but soon you will find that you have more than five things you are grateful for. It is just a matter of changing our habit of looking for faults and starting the habit of looking for things to be grateful for and to be happy about.

When you begin writing, start out with simple things, such as the following:

1. I am grateful that I woke up this morning.
2. I am grateful that I live with my family.
3. I am grateful that I have a job to go to.
4. I am grateful for my good health.

Soon you will be on a roll and can come up with more than five things to be grateful for.

In closing, remember to start your own daily gratitude diary or journal today! Make a habit of it and see how things start improving for you! The next tip to help you learn to be grateful is Tip #7, which is described below.

Happy Living Tip #7: Look at Common Daily Miracles with Childlike Wonder and Amazement!

Too often we take everything around us for granted and never really sit down and think about them. Each one of us can start to identify and think about some common daily occurrences that are truly magical. Then we will begin to truly appreciate the world and the Creator, which will pave the way to happy living.

Since there are hundreds of daily things that can cause us to wonder, I invite you, dear reader, to reflect on some of your own experiences. I had already talked about three common miracles in chapter 8. Here are some other daily miracles you can ponder on to start the ball rolling:

1. **Seed and the Tree:** How does the seed planted in the earth know just when conditions are right (enough water, soil, sun, etc.) to start germinating? Does it have sensors for water/food that allow it to grow roots? How does it know that the sun is above when it is buried in darkness? How does the seed of an apple tree only grow into an apple tree and not into an orange tree, etc.?

2. **Hatching Egg:** How does the liquid in an egg change into feathers, beak, and feet, and so on using just the warmth of a chicken or an incubator? Can we break an egg, remove the contents, and then change it into a chick (complete with feathers, eyes, feet, and so on) in a laboratory using only warmth?

3. **Flowers in a Pot:** How does a little earth and some water and some sunshine change into rainbow-colored flowers? Can we do the same in a science lab? By the way, isn't the rainbow itself an awesome miracle?

4. **Thoughts and Emotion:** What is an emotion? How can thoughts create emotions? Where exactly in our bodies do we feel the emotions? In the brain? In the heart? In the solar plexus? Or all over our bodies?

5. **Lizard on the Ceiling:** How does a lizard defy gravity by walking upside down on the ceiling and vertically on walls? Does it have suction cups on its feet? How do these suction cups release and re-grip alternately while it runs? Wouldn't it be great if we could imitate nature and invent such suction boots and gloves for the safety and efficiency of workers on high-rise buildings?

6. **Balance:** How do our ears manage to keep our balance while we are erect and prevent us from falling? Why is it more difficult to balance on one leg with the eyes shut?

7. **Coughing:** Think of all the complex actions that need to take place simultaneously before we can do something as commonplace as coughing. Now imagine and wonder about the thousands of other complex coordinated actions (such as sneezing, sleeping, immune system functions, digestion, respiration, etc.) that a body is capable of!

In life there are too many things to wonder about, to be amazed at in childlike curiosity, and to be grateful for. If only we would do it as a regular daily habit, then we will find happy living much easier to achieve.

Remember that it is nature that creates. Science merely tries to explain that which has been created. All of nature is a miracle!

This Happy Living Tip #7, namely "Pondering on Common Miracles," will automatically teach us gratitude and appreciation!

CHAPTER 17

How to Feel Upbeat and Energized

A lmost all of the tips in this book have focused on your thinking and how you can use it to create a happy state of mind—no matter what the circumstances! However, tips #8, #9, and #10 found in this chapter are very different.

*You don't have to do much thinking at all. Instead you **do** something that* immediately puts you in a happy frame of mind.

Happy Living Tip #8: Do Something Today to Make Someone Else Happy

Now doing something to make another person happy doesn't need to be a grandiose event that costs a large sum of money or a lot of time!

It can be as simple as a gesture of goodwill or as nice as a genuine smile or an enthusiastic "Good morning." It can be a heartfelt thank-you or a genuine word of appreciation to someone who has done you a good service.

It can also be some physical help like running simple errands, taking an ill neighbor to the clinic, or fetching a friend from the train station—anything that makes the other person happy. Even genuinely listening to what another person is saying instead of thinking about what we are going to say next is something that will make the other happy!

But it must be something that really will make the recipient happy and not just something that we think will make the person happy. Sometimes such actions can backfire because our assumptions can be wrong. For example, if you see a stranger having breakfast at a coffee shop and suddenly offer to pay the bill, he or she may act wary and suspicious of your gesture, assuming that you had some ulterior motive.

Underlying Principles

In all the earlier chapters we have learned that our thoughts create our moods or emotions. However, the reverse is also true! Our actions can also create our emotions and moods! The saying "Act enthusiastic, and you will feel enthusiastic!" is based on this fact.

However, this tip goes a little further to another universal principle. We attract that which we give out! If we give out affection, we get affection. If we give love, we get love in return, and if we give out anger, we get resentment and anger in return.

When we feel happy, we send out good vibrations, and so we attract good things into our life. This act of making someone else happy works to instantly uplift our own spirits!

If you don't believe me, just try it today. Just telephone a friend whom you have been meaning to call and have a friendly chat, or call your mother/father/sibling and tell him or her how much you love him or her!

See how uplifted you feel immediately after you make the call. So you have made two people happy with that one call—the receiver and yourself!

So remember this Happy Living Tip #8. Do something to make someone else happy! It is one of the easiest to implement and gets the fastest results!

*　　*　　*

Just the other day after a long delay and much procrastination, I finally managed to finish an article I had been intending to complete and submit to an e-zine. And when I finished it, I had a new burst of enthusiasm, a renewal of energy. I was so elated that I could not believe how happy I felt. I realized then that this could well be a great happy living tip as stated below.

Happy Living Tip #9: Complete a Long-Delayed Task or Chore

> *Just go ahead and finish something you have wanted to complete but have been putting off for some time.*

It does not matter how simple a task it is. Perhaps you have been wanting for days to clear your work desk of all the clutter. Perhaps you need to replace a hinge for your cabinet door. Perhaps you just need to run an errand for your spouse but have kept forgetting and postponing the task.

Whatever it is (no matter how mundane) when you get down to doing it and completing it, you will be rewarded with a joy that is totally out of proportion to the task you just performed!

I am sure that you, too, must have had this feeling of exuberance, satisfaction, and joy when you finally get down to it and complete a project or a job or even a chore.

This task you know you should complete would have been sitting at the back of your mind and niggling away constantly, bothering you to take some action. It may not have been uncomfortable enough to make you take action at once, but it would be irritating enough to keep you from enjoying your other activities.

*   *   *

Happy Living Tip #10: A Paradox of Happy Living, Namely Non-thinking

Throughout the pages of this book I seem to have only focused on how our minds and our thinking can help us achieve happy living. However, life being a paradox, in Tip #10, I am forced to write about the exact opposite: how non-thinking and not using our mind is one of the happier states of living that we can experience!

When I look back at my life, I find that some of the happiest occasions are when I am not thinking but doing something, when I am so engrossed in an action that I totally forget about the passage of time or the people around me.

This can happen whether at play or at work, although some of the examples I remember best happen during play:

- While I am playing a game of tennis, I am totally focused on the ball and nothing else during a prolonged exchange of shots back and forth. I am not thinking about the score, not thinking about winning or losing the point, not even thinking about where to play the next shot, but just hitting the ball instinctively and with absolute focus. When I am able to play like that, I find I am the happiest—no matter what the outcome of the game is, win or lose!

- Similarly during games of chess at home, there are times when I am so totally engrossed in the game that I have no idea that a couple of hours have passed. When we finish the game and I look around, only then do I realize that some friends have dropped by for a visit and gone; that I had drunk several cups of tea and had some biscuits my wife had set before me. I was so totally immersed in the game that I was not aware of anything else. By the way, those were the most enjoyable of games rather than the ones where I was constantly aware of the people and surroundings and thinking about the outcome of the game.

- During games of pool (billiards) on rare occasions when I am so absolutely focused on the game that I can see each ball so vividly and the table pockets seem as big as wash basins, so that I can pocket the balls from all angles. I just cannot miss on those days, and I end up beating the best player in the club!

- But this does not only happen during play. Sometimes when I am so involved in my work of technical writing, I really forget the passage of time and am not aware that it rained heavily for an hour or so or that it is way past my lunchtime. At such times I not only get a lot of work done but feel exhilarated when I am finished.

Thus, the gist of Happy Living Tip #10 is this:

Make time each day to live in the moment, to be exquisitely aware of the particular thing you are engaged in, just enjoying it and not thinking about anything, just experiencing it fully.

This can be as common a task as drinking a cup of coffee or cleaning dishes or writing a letter. Even in making love, non-thinking makes for more happiness than worrying about performance.

Thus, though it seems paradoxical, non-thinking living in the moment with absolute focus on your present action is just as natural a part of happy living as thinking and choosing to think happy thoughts are.

However, it would be impossible to live every moment of your life in such a way. For truly happy living on a daily basis, you would need to balance out these times of intense focused action with time for thinking—for dreaming, for planning, for nostalgia, for memories, and so on.

*   *   *

In this chapter we looked at tips #8, #9, and #10, where unlike most tips that ask us to use our mind, here we focus more on doing something to pep us up instantly. The next chapter deals with one of the most challenging issues we all face—that is, dealing with people harmoniously.

CHAPTER 18

Dealing with People

Since most of us find our greatest challenges in dealing with other people, this chapter provides five different tips for successful interpersonal communications. The tips for dealing with people are Tips #1, #11, #12, #13 and #14. Each of these is described in this chapter.

Happy Living Tip #1: Creating a Happiness Aura

I found Happy Living Tip #1, which is about creating a happiness aura, very useful when I had to attend a function to meet other people and work with them in a cordial atmosphere. This tip has already been detailed in chapter 10 under "Knowing the Nature of the Mind." Hence, we will not repeat it here.

*   *   *

Happy Living Tip #11: Stop Putting Labels on People

This is another vital tip on happy living. But because this particular tip has far-reaching effects on basic human relationships and interactions, I need to give you some background.

Many years ago when I was reading a book (where the central character was an antihero type), I realized that when we look at his life from that person's perspective, we are able to empathize with him and not just label him as a villain or a gangster and so on.

I also noticed the same thing happens when we are watching a movie, and we begin to root for the protagonist, even when he or she is not always perfect! For example, in the novel and the movie Godfather, we tend to empathize with the Don and do not just think of him merely as a mobster.

A more recent case of a movie we all appreciated even though it dealt with negative subjects (such as homophobia, adultery, murder, etc.) was American Beauty, which won an Oscar for that year. Here, too, we began to empathize with the characters without labeling them.

This insight led me to coin the phrase, "Separate the man from his actions, and you have cause to hate none!" This means that when we can differentiate the man from a particular action of his and not label him because of that action, then we are able to understand and accept him as a human being.

I used this insight in a practical way when I was bringing up my children. One of the rules I insisted on following and also told my wife to follow when it came to child discipline was this: Never tell a child, "You are a naughty kid! You are a bad boy/girl! You are good for nothing!" Instead say, "You are a good boy/girl, but what you did just now was bad!"

In other words, always let the child know that he or she is good and loved but that his or her behavior at that time was not good. My way of putting this into practice was as follows: Whenever I had occasion to reprimand a child, immediately after the punishment, I made it a point to show him that my love and affection for him was intact by giving him a treat (an ice cream or chocolate). I would clarify to the child, "You are a good boy, and I love you. But the action you did just now is not good or acceptable and that is why I had to scold/punish you!"

My wife used to say, "What kind of punishment is that? How will he ever feel the effect of the punishment if you immediately give him a treat?"

I explained, "Is punishment the main aim of the discipline? No! What is important is to see that he does not do those unacceptable things again! Now when a child knows he is loved and he is good, his self-image is intact, and he realizes the difference between himself (as a person) and his actions. He then knows that he can change his actions, and he will change voluntarily and not because of fear of punishment!"

So what has all this got to do with Happy Living Tip #11? Everything! In fact, it is the crux of the whole problem why we are unhappy in our interactions with other people—the inability to empathize with others because of the labels we place on them.

To take an extreme example, let us consider a master-slave relationship. The master feels the slave is less than human and so treats him as less than human. Different rules of behavior are considered acceptable if you are a master than if you are a slave! We all know that this is patently untrue and immoral. All human beings have the same rights and privileges and also the same responsibilities.

Because we came to understand this equality in humans, slavery has been abolished for almost one and a half centuries. Unfortunately this labeling of human beings still goes on in various guises.

- Most people look down on waiters, not realizing that they, too, are performing a service just as needed as that of a bank clerk or a manager or a doctor, etc. They seldom empathize with them. They don't think of the waiters as individual human beings because the label of *waiter* has somehow made them forget that these persons have feelings and aspirations. For all we know, the waiter may be just trying to earn money to pay his way through college, and that spirit of self-reliance is something that should be appreciated, not looked down upon!

- Here in Malaysia we hear of employers abusing their maids. They do not realize that the maid is also a human being with the same feelings as the employers. The maid, too, is a daughter or wife of someone who would be saddened to hear of the abuse his child or wife is undergoing. Most of all, the employers fail to realize that they too need the maid. She is an asset to running the household and does the jobs that the employer is not able to do or is not prepared to do. So the employer should be thankful that for less than a few hundred dollars a month he or she can employ a full-time maid. Instead employers use the label *maids* as though they are slaves.

- Even in a marriage, if we put labels on the couple as *only a husband* or *only the wife*, we are setting and expecting different standards of behavior for each without thinking of each as an individual first, and then only a husband or a wife. For example, a woman may be more comfortable working outside at a career, and the man could be someone who prefers to cook and keep home. But the labels placed on them by society may make them live truly miserable lives when they try to live up to the labels.

- So too, if a father labels his son/daughter as *only a child*, then he is not likely to listen to their genuine feelings/wishes/wants and will try to impose his own ideas on them—father-knows-best syndrome. This is the main reason for the so-called generation gap between parents and their kids.

So this happy living tip #11 says: *"Stop putting labels on people."*

When we label other people, we tend to dehumanize them to a lesser or greater degree. For example, we say things like "He's just a child," "She is just the maid," and so on, as though that label defines them as a person. This is totally untrue and unacceptable.

Nobody is just a child or just a waiter or just a wife or just a husband and so on. Each one is an individual human being with the same feelings and aspirations and the same rights to happiness as anyone else. Not understanding this or refusing to accept this is the major reason for unhappiness in human interactions.

When we stop labeling people, we begin to see the other person as an individual, and we respect his or her viewpoints and understand the reason for his or her actions even if we do not agree with those actions. Thus, we become less rigid in our outlooks. We don't criticize as we used to, and we don't get upset as we used to, which leads to happier relationships.

Some examples of how non-labeling can help us live happier lives are listed below:

1. **Parent-Child:** Even though born in the same home of the same parents, brought up in the same environment, fed the same food, and sent to the same schools, you will still find that each child is uniquely different! If the parent does not acknowledge this uniqueness, he or she may be guilty of bad comparisons between one child and the sibling:

    *   "Why can't you get good results at school?"
    *   "Why can't you play some manly sports instead of taking up music and dance?"
    *   "Why can't you be like your sister/brother?"

    The answer is that the child *cannot* be like his brother/sister because each child is uniquely different with his or her own talents, likes and dislikes! If we label all siblings as just kids, then we are not doing them justice, and they can end up with a lot of resentment, jealousy, envy, lack of good self-image, and so on. How then can the family life be happy? Only by stopping this practice of placing all children into one mold (i.e., by non-labeling)!

2. **Boss-Worker:** If the boss thinks of the employee as just a worker, at best he is unlikely to give enough respect or appreciation for the employee's work. At worst he may treat the employee badly, assuming that as a boss, he is above the law and his methods should not be questioned.

    Such a workplace is hell for the workers. If instead the boss empathized with his employees and treated each one as an individual, the office would be a happy place indeed and more efficient to boot.

3.   **Husband-Wife:** Recently I happened to watch an episode of *Oprah* where the wife of a politician who was involved in a scandal had this to say when she was asked if their marriage would survive, "We have been married for over twenty years, and he has been a devoted husband and father and also a friend to me all these years. Of course I am angry and feel betrayed now, but **can I define him by this one bad action of his?**" She had understood what I am trying to explain here—that an action does not define a person.

And there are many, many more such labels. You will be able to make up your own situations and think of the labels that you yourself use and see the folly of putting labels on people.

Then you will realize the truth in Happy Living Tip #11: Stop Putting Labels on People.

*   *   *

Happy Living Tip #12: Stop Trying to Convince Others

We know that beliefs are not absolute reality and are oftentimes replaced with new beliefs when we find that the old ones are incompatible with the reality of life and living. However, that does not mean we have to try to convince others to adopt our viewpoints.

We can always express our own views, but we should not expect others to think likewise. To keep trying to convert others to our beliefs is counterproductive to happiness (both theirs and ours). In other words, don't argue! As has been said by some wise person before, "A person convinced against his or her will is of the same opinion still."

So we cannot really change people's beliefs. They have to do it by themselves. It is only natural that we tend to treasure our old beliefs (even if they are probably mistaken) and we get somewhat upset when our beliefs are challenged. This is because we have invested a lot of time in either acquiring them or adopting them, and thus, these beliefs have become entrenched habits. So the key to good communication is to stop trying to convince others.

But the more important thing to notice (regarding happy living) is this: We do not feel good when we argue. Instead we feel angry. We feel upset, and we feel like retaliating and so on. Thus, arguing is not a happiness-inducing practice.

Does this mean that we should never speak out if our beliefs are different from that of others? Not at all! We can and should voice our thoughts and beliefs, but we must leave the choice of whether to accept it or not to the listeners!

If we follow the above rule, we would not get involved in futile arguments that only cause upset and unhappiness.

How am I qualified to talk about this? At one time my greatest weakness was that I liked to argue and try to force others to accept my views.

I argued about the news. I argued about movies. I argued about politics, about anything and everything. I needed to win the argument at all costs. This was very draining and stress-inducing for me and for those unfortunate enough to be within my earshot.

It took me a long time to realize that this type of behavior was antisocial and only caused because of my lack of good self-image. What a relief it was when I learned self-acceptance and did not need the approval of others to prop up my self-image.

I could still say what I truly felt without trying to force anyone to accept what I had to say. So I was free to express my views; and the listeners were free to choose whether my views made sense or not. That is how I came up with this quote, which was mentioned earlier:

> "I now accept that everyone is perfect at his or her own level of evolution. Hence, it makes no sense for me to try to convert anyone to my point of view. Let each one work out his or her individual evolutionary path."

So that is Happy Living Tip #12: Stop Trying to Convince Others!

*   *   *

Happy Living Tip #13: Compliment More, Criticize Less!

Now we come to another crucial tip in the fostering of good relationships, which was recently brought to my attention by my three-year-old granddaughter!

A couple of weeks ago when I visited my son, their eldest daughter (three-year-old Anya) asked me to help her with a jigsaw puzzle. I agreed and began putting some of the pieces together. Then I noticed that Anya was not doing anything to help and asked her to help. She replied, "Don't worry, Grandpa. You can do it!" She was quite happy to encourage me while she sat near and observed what I did.

When I finished, she exclaimed, "Grandpa, you are a genius!"

I was amazed to say the least. I had not expected a three-year-old to come up with such statements. Then I realized that my little granddaughter had used her wiles to get me to do her puzzle for her by encouragement and compliments.

Even though her compliments were over the top, yet it felt good to hear them. And whenever I thought about this incident, it brought a smile to my face and warmth to my heart.

The point is Anya knew what we adults seem to forget. We all love a compliment even if we know it is somewhat exaggerated (dare I say flattery). At the same time we hate criticism, no matter how well-intentioned.

However, most of us seem to practice the exact opposite. We are generous with our criticism and miserly with our praise!

For example, most men tend to keep quiet if their wives cook wonderful dinners, but if there was some little thing wrong with one of the dishes, they immediately criticize. Their excuse is that they are only trying to help her improve. How silly is that?

If instead they were to compliment their wife by saying, "Dinner was wonderful. You are a great cook!" The chances are she would try to do even better the next time.

People respond positively to encouragement and compliments, rather that criticism and complaints. This is just a fact of life. And this little three-year-old child understood human psychology and used it well to get what she wanted in a non-antagonistic way.

So that is a great happy living tip for us to follow: *Compliment more, and criticize less!*

In other words, in our relationships and dealings with others (no matter whether they are colleagues at work or family members or friends), we will be happier if we remembered the Happy Living Tip #13 above.

(It is a matter of never-ending amazement to me to see just how much I can learn from my interaction with my grandchildren. They are so full of fun, joy, and wisdom, if only we take the trouble to see.)

* * *

Happy Living Tip #14: Persuade Rather than Command

Whenever we want someone to do what we suggest, it is good to practice Happy Living Tip #14. This is especially useful when we are dealing with teenagers or other rebellious people. Always persuade rather than command. Let them feel it is in their own interest to do something.

This principle will be illustrated in the story below, which is an article I wrote long ago but never got around to publishing.

The Case of the Recalcitrant Calf

Your first response could be: "What the heck does recalcitrant mean?" Not to worry—the meaning will become clear when you read the story.

This story involves the famous writer (Emerson, I believe) who was holidaying at his farmhouse in the country. One fine day the great man found that a calf had wandered into his living room.

He first tried to shoo it away, but the calf had other ideas. He then called his son to help. The son tugged at the head while Emerson pushed at the rear, but the calf would not budge. They tried in vain for several minutes to get the calf outside and had just about given up.

Just then their milkmaid happened to pass by carrying a pail of milk, and they hailed her. She observed the situation calmly for a moment. She then dipped her thumb into the pail of milk, walked up to the calf, and placed her thumb in its mouth. The calf quietly followed her, busily sucking on her thumb. The maid and the hitherto recalcitrant calf made their exit.

Emerson was left nonplussed. For all his intellect and wit and wisdom, a mere chit of a girl had succeeded in doing easily what he and his son had failed to do.

The moral of the story is this: A calf or even people can be led but not driven. You do not need a doctorate to persuade others to do what you want, but you do need common sense. To lead someone we need to know what that person wants or needs. The same thing applies to parents and equally to children.

Now back to the big word. By now I'm sure you know that recalcitrant means stubborn intractable, refractory, or intransigent. Then why did I use the uncommon word instead of the common? Simply because we remember the uncommon words better. For example, how many of you know of the "son who wastes money"? But I'm sure all of you remember the story of "the prodigal son."

*   *   *

Of course it seems much easier to just command rather than to persuade, but you get better results with persuasion. The problem is persuasion needs some imagination; we need to understand what makes the other person tick, what he or she wants. We have to let them feel it is in their own interest to do something. If we just hope to get things done by browbeating others (especially our employees), our dealings with others will not be very happy.

In this chapter we looked at tips #11, #12, #13, and #14, which help us in our dealings with other people.

That brings us to part 5, the last part of the book, which tells about the actual practice of using the Joycentrix principles and the happy living tips with the help of a couple of case studies.

PART 5

Joycentrix System in Action

In part 4 we discussed several practical happy living tips based on the principles of the Joycentrix System.

In part 5 we go the next step and look at the Joycentrix System in action, namely case studies of people actually using the happy living tips and benefiting from them.

CHAPTER 19

Case Study #1:
My Own Experience

More than forty years ago I attended a Dale Carnegie public speaking course where I learned that when we want to communicate our ideas to others, the best way to do so is to use examples from our own personal experience. I have found that advice to be true not only in public speaking but also in writing. Hence, I shall begin part 5 with my personal experience in using the Joycentrix principles and the happy living tips.

For years I had been struggling with how to really live a happy life, being plagued by so-called wise sayings that stalked me night and day and brought me unnecessary worries. A small fraction of such sayings are mentioned below with my comments in parentheses:

- "Man proposes. God disposes!" (If that was really true, then there would be no point in us trying to do anything, for how can we puny humans go against the might of God? The saying should be changed to this: "Man proposes. God endorses!")

- "We are fated to experience this. It is our karma." (Perhaps it is fate or karma, but doesn't our free will have any power to affect our lives for the better in this lifetime?)

- "When good people suffer, it is because they are being tested by God." (What about bad people? Don't they get tested? Then why do I strive to be a good person? Is it to enter an unknown and imaginary heaven or avoid an equally imaginary hell after our death? Who guarantees these two extremes of reward and punishment? The religious teachers? How can we trust these people who claim to be the mouthpieces of God when no one has ever gone to heaven or hell and returned to tell the tale?)

- "This world is one of suffering!" (If that were true, then why do we celebrate birth and mourn death? Shouldn't it be the reverse?)

- "Money is the root of all evil." "It is easier for a camel to enter the eye of a needle than for a rich man to enter heaven!" (Does that mean that if I wished to be a good person, I should remain poor? Then why do churches and temples have collection boxes and actively ask for monetary contributions from their followers as well as donations from the rich?)

- "Desire is the starting point of all sorrow." (How can one achieve anything worthwhile in life without desire? In fact, the statement should read, "Desire is the starting point of all achievement!")

Because I had been bombarded continually with such seemingly wise sayings from revered sources, such as parents, religious teachers, and other enlightened persons, all through my childhood and teenage years, it was difficult for me to know whether I was making the right choices or not when I reached adulthood.

Fortunately for me, while in school, I had a strong intuitive belief in my ability to study and do well in school. Hence, I managed to do well in studies even though I never offered ritual prayers or offerings to the gods to help me do well. In fact, I was fortunate enough to be selected as scholar of the year in high school.

However, unlike others who had some strong ambition, I was never clear about what my passion in life was. I had always enjoyed studying, and I was curious about science, especially physics and chemistry. Hence, I got very good results in these subjects. So although I would have preferred to study philosophy, psychology, and literature, I was asked to continue in the science stream. This was how I ended up in the engineering profession.

Based on my high school results, I was offered several engineering scholarships. However, because I received the offer for electrical engineering first, I chose that as my future profession (as a result of the urging of my father). To put things in perspective, about one week after I had accepted the electrical engineering scholarship, I received one for mechanical engineering, and a week later I was offered a civil engineering scholarship. So my being in the electrical engineering field was due to random events rather than my own personal passion.

Because electrical engineering was not my passion, I never pursued it very vigorously, and while I was considered very competent at my work, I never achieved the heights I could have if my mind had been fully in it.

When I first began working and earning money, all the negative adopted beliefs about money that had resided in my subconscious began to kick in. Because of these false ideas regarding monetary success, I constantly sabotaged myself from ever becoming wealthy and successful materially.

It was only decades later that I realized just how damaging those beliefs (about money being evil and so on), adopted when I was just a child, had been on my career and worldly success. (This is perhaps the major reason why I am so vehemently against the teachers who taught me all the wrong things about life and living!)

Given below is just one example of how a strong negative belief can sabotage our best intentions. This example also shows how the laws of the mind are always neutral and why we need not blame karma, fate, or a lack of divine intervention for our problems in life.

How I Sabotaged Myself in a Real Estate Deal

Around 1980 just before the real estate boom began in Malaysia, when the Malaysian ringgit (RM) 2.50 was equivalent to one dollar in US currency, I booked a landed property (a corner double-story terrace house of about six thousand square feet valued at about RM54000) for only RM1000. I agreed to pay 10 percent of the value, or RM5400, when they began construction on the house. A couple of months later I received a letter from the developer saying that they were beginning construction soon and needed me to pay the 10 percent within one week if I wanted to retain booking of the property. The only difference was they said that the house was now valued at RM67000 and that I was supposed to pay up RM6700.

The alternative they offered was that if I wanted to give up my booking, they would pay me RM2000. Now no person in his right financial mind would have agreed to accept the RM2000 for the RM1000 initial booking fee, but I did! I made double my investment, which I spent immediately on a holiday.

Just three months after this incident, the same property I had given up earlier was sold to a buyer for RM130000. If I had just kept the property for a few months, I would have made about RM60000, which at that time would have been equivalent of about five years of income for me!

Analysis

So why did I do such a silly thing? I was not coerced by anyone into doing so. My reasoning is as follows: From very young I had been brainwashed into thinking of money as evil, initially by the Hindu scriptures that say, "Avoid all desires because they only bring sorrow," and then by my parents who unintentionally added to this idea by telling me stories of Vivekananda, Gandhi, Buddha, and so on (all of whom had renounced wealth). So the message was that in order to become great, man had to remain poor or renounce riches!

This idea that money was evil was further reinforced by my stint in a Catholic school where they taught me to disparage money saying that it would be 'easier for the camel to enter the eye of the needle than for a rich man to enter heaven'.

So at that impressionable age I had adopted the false belief that money was evil and being rich was bad! Later on when I grew up and knew better, this belief was already locked into my subconscious and kept sabotaging any conscious plans I had of creating wealth.

In the above case of my real estate deal, my mind being connected to the universal mind knew that if I kept that booking, I would become comparatively rich in a few months! *So in order to keep me poor (as commanded by my subconscious mind, which had overridden my conscious orders), I was tempted to choose a little easy money and lose out on a large sum.*

So the principle is the same: our minds attract what they are focused upon with the help of synchronicity in the universe, but whether we are able to benefit from the synergy or not is based on how our minds are wired up.

My conscious intentions had lined up a great way for me to get on the path to wealth, but the beliefs I had deep in my subconscious mind made me choose an action that kept me from that wealth.

That is why the beliefs we are taught at an early impressionable age are so powerful, and this knowledge is what religions use to manipulate the minds of children and consequently the adults.

When beliefs are ingrained in our minds as children, it is difficult to erase or replace them when we are adults. *It can be done but takes a lot of work to undo a habitual way of thinking.* This is what I am hoping to do with this book—to help people recognize their erroneous beliefs and slowly change these using simple, practical ways of retraining the mind.

Over the years I had tried numerous methods of earning extra income but always failed. When I had finally learned to make some money, I found that I could not keep it! I kept losing the money to hare-brained schemes that no thinking person would have got involved in.

Having a high IQ does not exempt us from failing miserably at financial dealings if we have the wrong financial beliefs. In my own case having a high IQ (being a qualified Mensa member) did not prevent me from acting stupidly when it came to financial investments.

*   *   *

Because I had wrong beliefs about the world and about GOD, when things went wrong (as they often will at the beginning of any new ventures), I began to be assailed with doubt.

I constantly worried whether the choices I made were indeed blessed by god or not, whether I had to perform prayers and pilgrimages before I embarked on any project to ensure their success; and so on. Obviously, such thinking ensured that I remained unsuccessful, unhappy, and frustrated!

My First Turning Point

The first turning point in my life was the day I formulated the first of my Joycentrix principles, which is the following: Believe in a Creator who is unconditionally loving and compassionate, not in one who is vindictive and vengeful!

Without this basic belief, my life was doomed to be one of continual drama, crisis, unhappiness, and misery. If I continued to fear GOD as a dictator and this world as a penitentiary, then there was no way I was going to be happy!

When I truly believed that GOD is a benevolent being, logically it followed that GOD and the universe are for me, not against me!

This belief was really the turning point in my life! No longer did I have to fear that GOD was constantly judging me and my actions and waiting to punish me in the hereafter. I could now joyfully begin to create the life I wanted without being plagued by doubt and always second-guessing myself.

I no longer felt miserable and helpless. I did not have to try in vain to appease an angry God with rituals, sacrifices, or prostrations, never knowing when I had done enough to please God.

No longer did I have to be God-fearing; instead I could become GOD-loving. Now my new mantra became "Man proposes. GOD endorses," and not, "Man proposes. God disposes," as I had been taught previously.

When I came to think of GOD, the Supreme Power as a most loving parent, one who encourages us in our endeavors, and forgives us our mistakes, the whole picture changed! I was able to live with a happy heart, go after my dreams with confidence, and truly live a joyful life. I had no more fear of the afterlife because I knew that a loving parent would have never created hell (a place of eternal punishment for our sins in a limited lifetime).

Also I do not fear death because I know I will be promoted to the next level in my evolution (or another dimension) in due course. I only need to concentrate on living a great and wonderful life while I am here, and my promotion is guaranteed!

In summary, you can easily imagine what a great weight had been lifted off my shoulders when I decided to believe in the Joycentrix principles 1 and 2. Before I had to keep wondering if I had made the right decision or not. Now I could confidently move forward, knowing that GOD and the universe would be working for me, not against me!

My Next Step Forward

The next step that helped me in my quest for a happier life was Joycentrix principle #3, which gave me confidence in the powers of my own mind (together with the universal mind), and Joycentrix principle #4, which helped me understand that (in spite of any personal limitations) I could still contribute to this world in my own unique way.

This gave me the confidence to search for my passion and purpose rather than just looking at ways to earn more income. I also learned a great truth—that when we follow our passion, the world uses precession to help us in our quest. What is precession? It is described below.

Precession and Buckminster Fuller

Precession is a word coined by one of the greatest of minds who lived in the twentieth century—Buckminster Fuller. He was one of our world's first futurists and global thinkers, and he was the inventor of the geodesic dome and dozens of other patents. Born in 1895, he was married at age twenty-two to Anne Hewlett. He encountered a lot of personal tragedies. In 1922, his first child died in his arms of pneumonia just a month before her fourth birthday after she had survived both infantile paralysis and spinal meningitis.

Five years later in 1927, his second daughter, Allegra, was born. It was the same year he went bankrupt and lost the company he had started with his father-in-law. Feeling totally depressed, he stood on the edge of Lake Michigan and contemplated suicide. It was then some inner voice told him, "You are not here in this world for yourself!"

Those words caused him to reevaluate his life and the world. From that day he decided to commit himself, his wife, and his infant daughter to solving world problems by designing artifacts that were capable of doing more with less.

He decided to pay no attention to earning a living, never promoting or selling or paying others to do so. He believed that if his designs were good for the world, then nature would take care of him by good *precession!*

How did it turn out? Well, he was well looked after by nature. He had owned forty-three cars, three planes, and several boats. Although Fuller never graduated from college, he was awarded nearly fifty honorary doctorates for his work in science and the humanities and more than a hundred major awards of merit, including the cover of *Time* in 1964. He died in 1983 at age eighty-eight. You can just Google his name to know more.

So what exactly is *precession*? In most small dictionaries you won't even find the word *precession*. On the Internet you can see some examples, but mostly it describes precession as related to geography and physics (about the rotation of the earth, gyroscopes, and so on.) The precession I'm talking about is that defined, studied, and practiced by Bucky himself for more than fifty years.

Simple examples of precession include the following:

- *Dropping a pebble into a lake.* When a pebble is dropped into a calm lake, as the pebble drops vertically downward to the bottom, it creates ripples, which travel outward horizontally away from where the pebble was dropped.

So in the above example, Bucky was referring to the fact that physically an action can create some ripples or side effects that are perpendicular to the direction of the action or movement. However, he took it a step further in the case below.

- *A bee gathering honey.* When a bee gathers honey (facing in one direction), pollen from the flower is being deposited on its legs (which are at right angles to its body). Thus, in the act of gathering honey, the bee unknowingly pollinates the flowers, thereby helping plant life to grow.

Bucky philosophized that the bee is getting a reward from nature because it is helping nature to reproduce plant life. So he theorized that if he himself were to do something to benefit the world, then he would always be well looked after and rewarded by the universe.

He believed that he need not live as most of us lived—always being worried about earning an income and surviving. As far as he was concerned, that philosophy worked out exceedingly well for him as you will know by reading of his accomplishments.

*   *   *

When I first read about this philosophy, I was more interested to know how I (a normal average human being) could put it into practice. How could I use precession to my advantage? As usual I analyzed the example Bucky gave of the bee gathering honey. I asked myself the following questions and got the following answers:

Question: "Does the bee know it is helping the universe in its task of preserving plant life?"

Answer: *No!*

Q: "Does the bee need to know that it is helping the universe in order to get its reward?"

A: *No! All it has to do is go after its desire or goal (to collect honey), and it will automatically be provided with its rewards.*

Similarly, I believed that we human beings are programmed for happiness by nature (or the universe or GOD). So all we have to do in order to get good precession is to go after our goals and dreams with a passion, knowing that when we pursue our purpose we are actually helping the universe in our own unique way!

Just think about it. If you are happy, you naturally spread this happiness. Your spouse is happy. Your children are happy. Your family is happy. Your office colleagues are happy to see you. If you are depressed, you spread your depression to all and sundry. A happy person does not get into fights or start wars. So it is vital to go after your own happiness.

Imagine what would happen if the bees had gone on strike and stopped gathering honey. The pollination of flowers would not take place, and plants would eventually die out. (This idea was explored a little in the movie *Bee Story*.) However, this won't happen because the bees are automatically programmed by nature to go out and gather honey, and they don't have a choice in the matter.

However, we humans have been given the choice either to follow our program and be happy or go against nature and be miserable!

If we keep saying that this world is only illusion and try to avoid living life to the fullest now, hoping somehow that will qualify us to live a better afterlife; then we are not unlike the bees that go on strike.

We are going against nature and GOD. Thus, if we persist in living a miserable life in this lifetime (which is against nature), we have no chance of being happier in the next life.

So my decision as an average person (not being Buckminster Fuller) to use precession was to go after my dreams with my whole heart and soul, knowing that the universe is for me. I will know if I am going in the right direction by the precession (or side effects) I create. If I have good precession, nature will give me a pat me on my shoulder by giving me lucky circumstances, and I will achieve success and happiness easily.

If, on the other hand, I am off track and create bad precession, then the same universe may give me a knock on the head rather than a pat on my shoulder to get me back on course again! Setbacks and lucky breaks are just nature's way of giving me both negative and positive feedback so that I can steer in the correct direction!

Each one of us is already creating our own reality. The only question is this: Are we happy with the life we are creating? We are free to choose our own beliefs and create our own reality. After all, that is what we are here on earth to do—live our own unique, individual life. If that creates good precession, well so much the better!

The Most Important Principle

While Joycentrix principles 1, 2, 3, and 4 were all important in providing me with a foundation for happy living, it was principle 5 that really helped me change my whole outlook on life. Knowing the truth about happiness, especially the first rule stating that happiness is a choice that I can make on a daily basis, began a wonderful change in me that helped in my relations with my wife and family and with colleagues and others.

Realizing that I could in fact choose happy thoughts to replace angry or unhappy thoughts was a real eye-opener for me. Before that I had believed like most of us that it was the actions of other people as well as external circumstances that caused me to be happy or unhappy.

Since it is just not possible to change the actions of everyone else, then happiness becomes an impossible goal. However, I have the power to change myself and my responses to other people. I also have the power to decide what thoughts occupy my mind, no matter what the circumstances.

When I realized these truths, I found I could be happier on a daily basis. An example was described in chapter 12 under the title "How I Overcame My Road Rage Almost Overnight."

The biggest insight I had regarding the fact that we alone control our thoughts was *that it felt good to think happy thoughts!* Every time I chose a better thought whenever I felt unhappy, angry, or vengeful, I immediately felt happier. After some time of practicing changing channels and choosing happier responses, this became habit, and I began to enjoy this new happy state of mind.

In fact, it felt really lousy to think angry thoughts or hateful thoughts or be argumentative or enact any of the other negative reactions I used to have. I ended up wondering how on earth I could have lived with such negative thoughts in my mind for long periods of time.

Let me repeat, *"It is we alone and no one else who controls what thoughts we allow to dwell in our minds, and it is the thoughts that we allow to stay in our minds that make for happiness or misery!"*

If the reader were to forget everything else I have said in this book and only remember this one truth, then he or she would be able to live a much happier life than what he or she is experiencing at present. To be able to choose our thoughts is one of the greatest powers that we have. It means we can respond to external circumstances exactly as we want to.

When we are criticized unfairly, we can choose to retaliate in anger or respond calmly and ask ourselves whether there is some truth in the criticism. If there is some truth in the criticism, then we can take steps to rectify the matter if possible. Either way, it is our own choice whether to escalate the problem or to resolve it.

When we come across a tragedy, say the loss of a loved one, we can choose either to think of how we are going to be affected by the loss and be miserable, or we can think of all the wonderful times we had together (which can never be lost) and also realize that the person has completed his or her lifetime here and gone on to another level of evolution. Thus, we can choose either to mourn inconsolably or accept the loss peacefully while we retain all the fond memories.

If we were to be laid off from work suddenly, we can choose either to dwell on how unjust the company is and complain about the situation and remain steeped in self-pity, or we can be grateful for whatever we do have, such as our ability, our health, our friends, and our influence. We can also think that it is all for the best, believing that there is a better opportunity waiting for us out there, and this was just the prod we needed to take the first step to a better future!

Thus, whatever the situation we have to face, if we believe that we can choose our own thoughts; then we can do so, thereby retaining a happy outlook on life.

CHAPTER 20

Case Study #2: Saving a Marriage Headed for the Rocks

F irst of all, let me state that staying happy in a marriage is vastly different from just staying in a marriage!

It is a statistical fact that more marriages in the West end up in divorce than in the East. However, it does not mean that most couples in the East who remain married are happy! Many married couples are living lives of quiet desperation because Eastern culture places a lot of value on self-sacrifice. Hence, unhappy couples stay together for reasons that include the following:

- "We don't want our children to suffer the loss of a parent."
- "We can't do much about it. We just have to accept it as fate."
- "What will the people say?"

Public view of female divorcees is also very negative in the East (in typical male chauvinistic fashion).

So because the divorce ratio in the East is less, that does not mean the marriages are happy. But it does not have to be like that!

It is possible to stay happy in our marriage if we know the secret. The secret is simple, but it takes discipline and effort to implement. Before I reveal the secret, let me tell you a story—a true story but with names changed to protect their privacy.

The Marriage Woes of Sham and Meena

Sham and Meena had an arranged marriage. Basically both were good and honest people with many sterling qualities, but they differed greatly in their outlooks on life. Sham was more of a dreamer while Meena was a very practical woman who was bound by traditions.

He loved reading books and seeing movies, and he generally lived in the mind world of ideas while she was bored with movies or books. She did not consider them real. She preferred talking to friends about people and real things—like who had gotten married, who was expecting children, who had gotten promotions, and so on. Sham had another word for that reality. He called it gossip.

Meena's memory for facts about people and their relationships was incredible. She could remember which niece's son was studying what subjects in what school, which uncle's daughter was getting married to who, what their occupations were, and so on.

Sham, on the other hand, had an incredible memory too. He remembered movie stories, including the names of actors and actresses. He remembered inspiring quotations, ideas, and so on. He could be moved to laughter and tears by books and movies, but unlike Meena, he was not very affected by actual funerals or weddings of relatives!

Meena believed in ritual prayer. She fasted once per week and loved to attend temple functions and recite *bajans* (hymns) in Sanskrit, which she did not understand. Sham believed that since God was everywhere and understood all languages, why should he bother to go to temples and pray in certain approved sacred languages? He might as well pray at home and directly to God without using an intermediary.

As you can see, Sham and Meena were hardly the most compatible of couples! But their basic human values were the same: integrity, honesty, kindness, and so on. Both loved children and would never hurt them. Both were very honest with each other—sometimes too honest.

So they stayed together for years for all the wrong reasons stated above, always unhappy at perceived slights and uncaring—needing only the most trivial of incidents to start another argument, bringing up past grievances and adding to their misery.

Each one felt that the other was uncaring and unsupportive and tried to prove the other was at fault. Thus, there could be no solution until they realized that changing another is an impossible task and one can only change oneself.

When a brother suggested to Sham that he should be the one to make the change (because he was the one who enjoyed ideas and thinking and so on), Sham asked, "Why should I alone attempt to change myself? Doesn't it take two hands to clap? Isn't marriage a partnership? Why should I alone be giving in?"

So Sham and Meena were always unhappy—angry with each other and just waiting to find fault with each other. As the saying goes, "What we focus on expands!" So when each looked for faults in the other, they found it aplenty.

So much so that their teenage son asked years ago, "Why do you two stay together if you are fighting all the time? Why don't you try separation?"

Is there any hope of saving such a marriage?

Strangely enough, in spite of their incompatibility, their marriage did survive. How? What was their secret? That is revealed below.

One day while Sham was listening to a meditation tape, he had an epiphany: "If I refuse to change my own perceptions, even if I were to get divorced and remarry, the problem would still be there because it all begins with my own lack of acceptance that my spouse can have a different set of beliefs."

Sham finally decided that if there was to be any change in the relationship, it had to come from him! Initially he had been reluctant to do so because he believed in 'equality' in a marriage.

Finally he realized that it was not a contest of who was right but an attempt to make a relationship work. He found that it was not necessary for both the people in a relationship to make a change at the same time!

Even if he alone were to begin to make changes in himself, then the relationship could be salvaged. And between himself and Meena, he was the better candidate for change since he read a lot, thought a lot, and was interested in change.

So he started with learning to truly accept himself with all his weaknesses and strengths. He did the mirror exercise regularly and began to truly love himself as an individual, a unique human being.

When he could truly love himself, he realized that he could love Meena too (without being judgmental). He began to look for the good that Meena did instead of what she failed to do! Thus, he was able to find many things he had been taking for granted and not showing appreciation for.

When his younger colleagues at the office kept getting calls from their wives regarding problems at home, he realized that Meena had never called him at the office to complain about anything.

He could even go away on business trips for a couple of days without any worry unlike his colleagues, who kept getting constant calls from their homes.

Meena cooked well, looked after their three active children, and kept the house spic and span without any complaints—all without a maid.

Once he began to appreciate what was good about Meena, Sham stopped criticizing her for every little thing! He could then truly love her for being herself and the good she did.

This was a great relief for Meena. It took away the tension she felt of always being judged, and so she reciprocated. She began to feel that Sham really cared for her, and so she was more affectionate and loving too.

Fast forward many years to the present! Sham and Meena have now been married for more than thirty years. They have three children and grandchildren, and they are both really happy in their marriage (which even their son had expected to crash on the rocks!)

What was the secret that saved their marriage in spite of the myriad problems?

The secret can be spelled out as follows: self-acceptance and thereby unconditional acceptance of one's spouse. A brief analysis of why this works (written in the first person to help readers understand easily) is given below.

Self-Acceptance

Self-acceptance is vital. If I cannot accept myself just as I am with all my strengths and weaknesses, with my quirks and foibles, then how can I respect and love myself? If I am unable to love myself, how can I love others? Also, if I feel unlovable, how can others love me?

How true! If we cannot be at peace with our own inner selves, it makes no difference where we go to look for peace and happiness because we won't find it.

On the other hand, if we can accept and love ourselves unconditionally, we are happy within ourselves. Then we find it easy to love others just the way they are. If we feel happy inside, we send out good vibrations, and therefore, others react to us in a good way.

Thus unconditional love starts from inside us and spreads outward to our spouse, our children, our friends, and our colleagues at work.

Unconditional Acceptance of Spouse

If I accept my spouse just as she is, I will not be critical of her and be forever trying to change her. This impulse to try to change the other is, I believe, the number-one cause of unhappiness in a marriage. Of course, other external circumstances, such as financial problems, will also contribute to the unhappiness.

But this non-acceptance of the spouse as he or she is remains the main cause of marital misery. If I don't accept my wife and love her without being judgmental, I cannot focus on all her good qualities. Instead I will always be harping on her negatives, and who enjoys being nagged at?

Once I accept my wife unconditionally without judgment, I begin to appreciate all her good qualities. When I begin accepting and stop expecting her to react in a particular way and allow her to be herself, things that used to upset me will not bother me anymore. In fact, I can even have a fondness for those very foibles (that used to annoy me) because I appreciate that is what makes her unique.

What a great turnaround? That which used to annoy and irritate us about the spouse's mannerisms and behavior are now accepted (even welcomed) as a parts of her or his unique personality!

Conclusion

Thus even in cases of extreme incompatibility (as in Sham and Meena's case), it is possible to stay happy in a marriage. All that needs to be done is for at least one of the partners to act on the following:

- Begin to accept the other unconditionally as a unique, special being.
- Look for the good in the other.
- Don't expect the responses of the other to be the same as yours.
- Stop trying to change the other by nagging.
- Stop holding a judgmental attitude against the other.

This leads to genuine appreciation of the partner, which is one of the prerequisites of a happy partnership. If one partner will do that, over time the other cannot help but reciprocate, thereby leading to a happy marriage.

I would like to conclude this story with an insight of mine which I had some time ago, because it seems so relevant to this case:

> *"I understand and accept that each one of us is at a different stage of evolution and can have beliefs that may be totally at variance with mine. Thus, it makes no sense for me to get upset or angry at another if his or her beliefs do not agree with mine!"*

CHAPTER 21

Case Study #3: Example of Happiness Enhancers

To recap, happiness enhancers are what I call the second phase of happy living!

Phase 1 of happy living was all about *how to be happy in spite of circumstances* by controlling our thoughts and hence our feelings.

Phase 2 of happy living is about *how to change circumstances to suit us better* so that we can increase the happiness that we already have.

One of the fastest and easiest of ways to enhance your happiness is by setting a new goal for yourself!

Have you been just toying with an idea, a wish, or a daydream but never actually put your mind to it? Then setting a new goal is an ideal way to motivate yourself to act and start the process of achieving your goal.

Once you set a goal with a time line for its achievement, then immediately you feel energized with lots of ideas flooding your mind on how to go about achieving that goal. You will get a new motivation and an excitement you never felt before!

A story will best illustrate how setting a goal and going for it will increase your happiness.

Arun: The Little Boy Who Believed He Could

Even when he was a little boy, the word cannot was not in Arun's vocabulary! It never occurred to him that he could not get what he wanted all the time. He just went ahead and started doing things on the assumption that he could achieve it.

When he was just six years old, he decided he wanted an aquarium to keep some fish in. His parents were totally against the idea, and so was his elder brother. Mother explained why it was not good to keep a living thing in captivity. Father explained how much work it was to maintain an aquarium, and his brother told him that it was bad luck. After he listened patiently to each of their objections, Arun said, "So when can we get the aquarium?"

He had listened, but his mind was already made up. And in his imagination he already had his aquarium. But the rest of the family were adamant and refused to buy him one! So he brought out his meager savings of a few dollars and gave it to his father, asking him to get the smallest one that could be bought with the money.

Now the parents felt sorry for the six-year-old boy (as any parent would) and decided to get him a slightly bigger one. A few months later (in spite of the early unanimous opposition of all the family), there was a full-sized aquarium in the house! This trait of never expecting to fail continued to develop as Arun grew up. The parents called it obstinacy at that time, but now they realize that it was another term for persistence and conviction.

When Arun was in his teens, he was crazy about becoming a pilot. Whenever he accompanied his parents to the airport to send off family members, he insisted on lingering to watch the big 747 jets take off. He must have been imagining himself flying those jets.

A few years later he had a basic degree in computer science, but he was not at all keen on pursuing computer science as a career. He had not forgotten about his dream. He applied to the local airlines to become a cadet pilot but was turned down by Malaysian Airlines (MAS) since his high school results were not good enough. Then he found that Singapore Airlines (SIA) was not that particular about his high school results and would accept a first degree for consideration as a cadet pilot.

Before he went for the first aptitude test and the subsequent interviews, he prepared himself by reading up about jet planes (though he normally hated reading of any kind). He also managed to contact other pilots by getting assistance from a most unlikely source! For instance, his mother used to go for walks every morning, and her walking buddies knew someone whose son was a pilot.

To cut the story short, Arun is now a pilot with SIA and flying 747 jets, and he has been able to enhance his happiness tremendously! He now has his own family with a wife and a two-year-old child. He owns a couple of houses and a luxury car as well, and he is not thirty years old yet.

Analysis

Arun was able to increase or enhance his happiness because he set a goal for himself and went for it despite all the hurdles he had to overcome. He achieved his dream because he never took no for an answer and did whatever was necessary in the pursuit of his goal.

However, I must point out that Arun was basically already a happy person, which is a prerequisite to enhancing one's happiness. He seldom complained about others. Instead he seemed to accept others unconditionally. As an example, although he himself never even smoked, while he was in college he had a roommate who took drugs! But it didn't seem to bother Arun. He said to himself, "That is his choice, so why should I be upset?"

This trait is in fact one I have written about in the Happy Living Tip #4 (self-acceptance and the acceptance of others), which is another one of the requisites for happy living phase one.

In the story above, Arun's never-take-no-for-an-answer attitude is a practical example of the first two Joycentrix principles of happy living in action, namely trusting that GOD is for us and the universe is also for us and not against us.

What we desire intensely in our innermost heart is also what GOD desires for us and what the universe will conspire to make real. Unfortunately most of us have been taught to believe the opposite.

We limit ourselves by believing that the universe is basically unfriendly to us and that we need to appeal to GOD to give us permission to go after our dreams.

We are taught to believe that man proposes and God disposes! If that were really true and GOD was against us, then we humans could never succeed at anything. Such erroneous thinking is reflected in our own reality, whereby we seldom achieve our goals.

So the secret behind this happiness enhancer is to remember to set new goals and go after your dreams confidently, not tentatively! Knowing that GOD and the universe are for you helps you realize your innermost desires and dreams easily.

CONCLUSION

We have now come to the end of this little book on how to make happy living a daily way of life. Below is a summary of what we have learned so far:

- First of all we have explored what real happiness is as opposed to pseudo happiness.

- Next we have learned how it is our innermost beliefs that help create our own reality—that it is not just because of random external circumstances. Above all we have learned that having the correct (more positive) beliefs about the world, about GOD, and about the universe will help us achieve our ultimate purpose in life—that is to live joyfully and spread joy.

- More importantly we now know that we have complete control of what thoughts we allow to occupy our mind. Since our thoughts create our feelings and emotions, we can control our feelings and emotions by choosing different, more empowering thoughts.

- We can do this by becoming aware at each instant just what thoughts we are allowing to dwell in our mind. Once we are aware of our own self-defeating thoughts and emotions, we can choose to change these to what will make us happy instead of hanging on to that which is keeping us mired in misery.

- We have also explored the difference between happiness and happiness enhancers!

Before you close this book, I would like to impress upon you, the reader one supremely important issue. *The purpose of all our thoughts, words, and actions is always **to experience feelings**.* In fact, the purpose of all life is feelings! Without feelings, none of the thoughts, words, deeds, or experiences can mean anything to us. For example:

- I can say, "Waking up each morning is a daily miracle," but until and unless I really and truly feel it and experience the euphoria that such a realization brings, these remain mere words.

- Someone could say, "The mango tastes sweet," but until we ourselves have tasted the mango and felt its sweetness, those are just words.

- Similarly we may say, "To forgive is divine"; but until we really practice forgiving, we cannot experience the joy and peace it can give us.

You may accept these words intellectually, but it is only when you truly feel and experience them that these words can have any value to you. This applies to all the principles of the Joycentrix System as well as the numerous happy living tips I have included in this book.

Each one of them is only useful when we really feel the emotions associated with them. For example, consider the following:

- The mirror exercise will mean nothing until we truly learn the feeling of self-acceptance.

- The changing channels technique will only work if we begin to feel love when we think of our pets or our children, thereby changing our moods.

- If you say, "I believe in a benevolent GOD," and still worry about the twin fantasies of hell and heaven, it only means you do not yet feel the benevolence of GOD.

- A motivational guru may have told you that you can and will achieve your deepest desires! But until you truly feel in your heart of hearts that GOD and the world are for you and not against you, you will be doomed to fail because you would be going after your goals with trepidation and fear!

- Saying, "Bless you," works because we feel the positive vibrations of the word bless as opposed to the negative vibrations we feel when we say, "Curse you."

So my final word to you, dear reader, is this: Remember that life is all about feelings and the best experience of all is feeling good, namely feeling love, appreciation, gratitude, and joy!